THE COMMUNIST MANIFESTO

A MODERN EDITION

THE COMMUNIST MANIFESTO

A MODERN EDITION

◆

KARL MARX

AND

FREDERICK ENGELS

WITH AN INTRODUCTION BY
ERIC HOBSBAWM

VERSO

London • New York

This paperback edition first published by Verso 2012
© Verso 2012
First published in hardback by Verso 1998
Introduction © Eric Hobsbawm 2012
Manifesto of the Communist Party first published in English 1848;
this translation first published 1888

5 7 9 10 8 6 4

Verso
UK: 6 Meard Street, London W1F 0EG
US: 20 Jay Street, Suite 1010, Brooklyn, NY 11201
www.versobooks.com

Verso is the imprint of New Left Books

ISBN-13: 978-1-84467-876-1

British Library Cataloguing in Publication Data
A catalogue record for this book is available from the British Library

Library of Congress Cataloging-in-Publication Data
A catalog record for this book is available from the Library of Congress

Typeset by M Rules
Printed in the UK by CPI Group (UK) Ltd,
Croydon CR0 4YY

CONTENTS

INTRODUCTION

Eric Hobsbawm

I

In the spring of 1847 Karl Marx and Frederick Engels agreed to join the so-called League of the Just [*Bund der Gerechten*], an offshoot of the earlier League of the Outlaws [*Bund der Geächteten*], a revolutionary secret society formed in Paris in the 1830s under French Revolutionary influence by German journeymen – mostly tailors and woodworkers – and still mainly composed of such expatriate artisan radicals. The League, convinced by their 'critical communism', offered to publish a Manifesto drafted by Marx and Engels as its policy document, and also to modernize its organization along their lines. Indeed, it was so reorganized in the summer of 1847, renamed League of the Communists [*Bund der Kommunisten*], and committed to the object of 'the overthrow of the bourgeoisie, the rule of the proletariat, the ending of the old society which rests on class contradiction [*Klassengegensätzen*] and the establishment of a new society without classes or private property'. A second congress of the League, also held in London in November–December

1847, formally accepted the objects and new statutes, and invited Marx and Engels to draft the new Manifesto expounding the League's aims and policies.

Although both Marx and Engels prepared drafts, and the document clearly represents the joint views of both, the final text was almost certainly written by Marx – after a stiff reminder by the Executive, for Marx, then as later, found it hard to complete his texts except under the pressure of a firm deadline. The virtual absence of early drafts might suggest that it was written rapidly.[1] The resulting document of twenty-three pages, entitled *Manifesto of the Communist Party* (more generally known since 1872 as *The Communist Manifesto*), was 'published in February 1848', printed in the office of the Workers' Educational Association (better known as the *Communistischer Arbeiterbildungsverein*, which survived until 1914), at 46 Liverpool Street in the City of London.

This small pamphlet is by far the most influential single piece of political writing since the French Revolutionary *Declaration of the Rights of Man and Citizen*. By good luck it hit the streets only a week or two before the outbreak of the revolutions of 1848, which spread like a forest fire from Paris across the continent of Europe. Although its horizon was firmly international – the first edition hopefully, but wrongly, announced the impending publication of the Manifesto in English, French, Italian, Flemish and Danish – its initial impact was exclusively German. Small though the Communist League was, it played a not insignificant part

---

[1]   Only two items of such material have been discovered – a plan for Section III and one draft page. Karl Marx–Frederick Engels, *Collected Works*, vol. 6 (London 1976), pp. 576–7.

in the German Revolution, not least through the newspaper *Neue Rheinische Zeitung* (1848–49), which Karl Marx edited. The first edition of the Manifesto was reprinted three times in a few months, serialized in the *Deutsche Londoner Zeitung*, corrected and reset in thirty pages in April or May 1848, but dropped out of sight with the failure of the 1848 revolutions. By the time Marx settled down to his lifelong exile in England in 1849, the Manifesto had become sufficiently scarce for him to think it worth reprinting Section III ('Socialistische und kommunistische Literatur') in the last issue of his London magazine *Neue Rheinische Zeitung, politisch-ökonomische Revue* (November 1850), which had hardly any readers.

Nobody would have predicted a remarkable future for the Manifesto in the 1850s and early 1860s. A small new edition was privately issued in London by a German *émigré* printer, probably in 1864, and another small edition in Berlin in 1866 – the first ever actually published in Germany. Between 1848 and 1868 there seem to have been no translations apart from a Swedish version, probably published at the end of 1848, and an English one in 1850, significant in the bibliographical history of the Manifesto only because the translator seems to have consulted Marx – or (since she lived in Lancashire) more probably Engels. Both versions sank without trace. By the mid-1860s virtually nothing that Marx had written in the past was any longer in print.

Marx's prominence in the International Working Men's Association (the so-called 'First International', 1864–72) and the emergence, in Germany, of two important working-class parties, both founded by former members of the Communist League who held him in high esteem, led to a revival of interest in the Manifesto, as in his other writings. In particular, his eloquent defence of the Paris Commune of 1871 (commonly known as *The Civil War in France*) gave him considerable notoriety in the press as a dangerous leader of international subversion, feared by governments. More specifically, the treason trial of the German Social-Democratic leaders, Wilhelm Liebknecht, August Bebel and Adolf Hepner in March 1872 gave the document unexpected publicity. The prosecution read the text of the Manifesto into the court record, and thus gave the Social-Democrats their first chance of publishing it legally, and in a large print run, as part of the court proceedings. As it was clear that a document published before the 1848 Revolution might need some updating and explanatory commentary, Marx and Engels produced the first of the series of prefaces which have since usually accompanied new editions of the Manifesto.[2] For legal reasons the preface could not be widely distributed at the time, but in fact the 1872 edition (based on the 1866 edition) became the foundation of all subsequent editions. Meanwhile, between 1871 and 1873, at least nine editions of the Manifesto appeared in six languages.

Over the next forty years the Manifesto conquered the world, carried forward by the rise of the new (socialist) labour parties, in which the Marxist influence rapidly increased in the 1880s. None of these chose to be known as a Communist Party until the Russian Bolsheviks returned to the original title after the October Revolution, but the title *Manifesto*

---

[2]   In the lifetime of the founders they were: (1) Preface to the (second) German edition, 1872; (2) Preface to the (second) Russian edition, 1882 – the first Russian translation, by Bakunin, had appeared in 1869, understandably without Marx's and Engels's blessing; (3) Preface to the (third) German edition, 1883; (4) Preface to the English edition, 1888; (5) Preface to the (fourth) German edition, 1890; (6) Preface to the Polish edition, 1892; and (7) Preface 'To Italian Readers', 1893.

of the Communist Party remained unchanged. Even before the Russian Revolution of 1917 it had been issued in several hundred editions in some thirty languages, including three editions in Japanese and one in Chinese. Nevertheless, its main region of influence was the central belt of Europe, stretching from France in the West to Russia in the East. Not surprisingly, the largest number of editions were in the Russian language (70) plus 35 more in the languages of the Tsarist empire – 11 in Polish, 7 in Yiddish, 6 in Finnish, 5 in Ukrainian, 4 in Georgian, 2 in Armenian. There were 55 editions in German plus, for the Habsburg Empire, another 9 in Hungarian and 8 in Czech (but only 3 in Croat and one each in Slovak and Slovene), 34 in English (covering the USA also, where the first translation appeared in 1871), 26 in French and 11 in Italian – the first not until 1889.[3] Its impact in southwestern Europe was small – 6 editions in Spanish (including the Latin American ones); one in Portuguese. So was its impact in southeastern Europe (7 editions in Bulgarian, 4 in Serb, 4 in Romanian, and a single edition in Ladino, presumably published in Salonica). Northern Europe was moderately well represented, with 6 editions in Danish, 5 in Swedish and 2 in Norwegian.[4]

This uneven geographical distribution did not only reflect the uneven development of the socialist movement, and of Marx's own influence, as distinct from other revolutionary ideologies such as anarchism. It should also remind us that there was no strong correlation between the size and

[3] Paolo Favilli, *Storia del marxismo italiano. Dalle origini alla grande guerra* (Milan 1996), pp. 252–4.
[4] I rely on the figures in the invaluable Bert Andréas, *Le Manifeste Communiste de Marx et Engels. Histoire et Bibliographie 1848–1918* (Milan 1963).

power of social-democratic and labour parties and the circulation of the Manifesto. Thus until 1905 the German Social-Democratic Party (SPD), with its hundreds of thousands of members and millions of voters, published new editions of the Manifesto in print runs of not more than 2,000–3,000 copies. The party's *Erfurt Programme* of 1891 was published in 120,000 copies, while it appears to have published not many more than 16,000 copies of the Manifesto in the eleven years 1895 to 1905, the year in which the circulation of its theoretical journal, *Die Neue Zeit*, was 6,400.[5] The average member of a mass Marxist social-democratic party was not expected to pass examinations in theory. Conversely, the 70 pre-Revolutionary Russian editions represented a combination of organizations, illegal for most of the time, whose total membership cannot have exceeded a few thousand. Similarly, the 34 English editions were published by and for the scattering of Marxist sects in the Anglo-Saxon world, operating on the left flank of such labour and socialist parties as existed. This was the milieu in which 'the clearness of a comrade could be gauged invariably from the number of earmarks on his *Manifesto*'.[6] In short, the readers of the Manifesto, though they were part of the new and rising socialist labour parties and movements, were almost certainly not a representative sample of their membership. They were men and women with a special interest in the theory that underlay such movements. This is probably still the case.

---

[5]   Data from the annual reports of the SPD *Parteitage*. However, no numerical data about theoretical publications are given for 1899 and 1900.

[6]   Robert R. LaMonte, 'The New Intellectuals', *New Review* II, 1914; cited in Paul Buhle, *Marxism in the USA: From 1870 to the Present Day* (London 1987), p. 56.

This situation changed after the October Revolution – at all events, in the Communist Parties. Unlike the mass parties of the Second International (1889–1914), those of the Third (1919–43) expected all their members to understand – or at least to show some knowledge of – Marxist theory. The dichotomy between effective political leaders, uninterested in writing books, and the 'theorists' like Karl Kautsky – known and respected as such, but not as practical political decision-makers – faded away. Following Lenin, all leaders were now supposed to be important theorists, since all political decisions were justified on grounds of Marxist analysis – or, more probably, by reference to the textual authority of 'the classics': Marx, Engels, Lenin and, in due course, Stalin. The publication and popular distribution of Marx's and Engels's texts therefore became far more central to the movement than they had been in the days of the Second International. They ranged from series of the shorter writings, probably pioneered by the German *Elementarbücher des Kommunismus* during the Weimar Republic, and suitably selected compendia of readings, such as the invaluable *Selected Correspondence of Marx and Engels*, to *Selected Works* of Marx and Engels in two – later three – volumes, and the preparation of their *Collected Works* [*Gesamtausgabe*]; all backed by the – for these purposes – unlimited resources of the Soviet Communist Party, and often printed in the Soviet Union in a variety of foreign languages.

The Communist Manifesto benefited from this new situation in three ways. Its circulation undoubtedly grew. The cheap edition published in 1932 by the official publishing houses of the American and British Communist Parties in 'hundreds of thousands' of copies has been described as 'probably the largest mass edition ever issued in

English'.[7] Its title was no longer a historical survival, but now linked it directly to current politics. Since a major state now claimed to represent Marxist ideology, the Manifesto's standing as a text in political science was reinforced, and it accordingly entered the teaching programme of universities, destined to expand rapidly after the Second World War, where the Marxism of intellectual readers was to find its most enthusiastic public in the 1960s and 1970s.

The USSR emerged from the Second World War as one of the two superpowers, heading a vast region of Communist states and dependencies. Western Communist Parties (with the notable exception of the German Party) emerged from it stronger than they had ever been or were likely to be. Although the Cold War had begun, in the year of its centenary the Manifesto was no longer published simply by communist or other Marxist editors, but in large editions by non-political publishers with introductions by prominent academics. In short, it was no longer only a classic Marxist document – it had become a political classic *tout court*.

It remains one, even after the end of Soviet communism and the decline of Marxist parties and movements in many parts of the world. In states without censorship, almost certainly anyone within reach of a good bookshop, and certainly within reach of a good library, can have access to it. The object of a new edition is therefore not so much to make the text of this astonishing masterpiece available, and still less to revisit a century of doctrinal debates about the 'correct' interpretation of this fundamental document of Marxism. It is to remind ourselves that the

---

[7]   Hal Draper, *The Annotated Communist Manifesto* (Center for Socialist History, Berkeley, CA 1984), p. 64.

Manifesto still has plenty to say to the world in the first decades of the twenty-first century.

II

What does it have to say?

It is, of course, a document written for a particular moment in history. Some of it became obsolete almost immediately – for instance, the tactics recommended for Communists in Germany, which were not those in fact applied by them during the 1848 Revolution and its after-math. More of it became obsolete as the time separating the readers from the date of writing lengthened. Guizot and Metternich have long retired from leading governments into history books; the Tsar (though not the Pope) no longer exists. As for the discussion of 'Socialist and Communist Literature', Marx and Engels themselves admitted in 1872 that even then it was out of date.

More to the point: with the lapse of time, the language of the Manifesto was no longer that of its readers. For example, much has been made of the phrase that the advance of bourgeois society had rescued 'a consider-able part of the population from the idiocy of rural life'. But while there is no doubt that Marx at this time shared the usual townsman's contempt for – as well as ignorance of – the peasant milieu, the actual and analyti-cally more interesting German phrase ('dem Idiotismus des Landlebens entrissen') referred not to 'stupidity' but to 'the narrow horizons', or 'the isolation from the wider society', in which people in the country-side lived. It echoed the original meaning of the Greek term 'idiotes', from which the current meaning of 'idiot' or 'idiocy' is derived: 'a person concerned only with his own private affairs and not with those

of the wider community'. In the course of the decades since the 1840s
– and in movements whose members, unlike Marx, were not classically
educated – the original sense had evaporated, and was misread.

This is even more evident in the Manifesto's political vocabu-
lary. Terms such as 'Stand' ('estate'), 'Demokratie' ('democracy') or
'Nation/national' either have little application to late-twentieth-century
politics, or no longer retain the meaning they had in the political or
philosophical discourse of the 1840s. To take an obvious example: the
'Communist Party' whose Manifesto our text claimed to be had nothing
to do with the parties of modern democratic politics, or the 'vanguard
parties' of Leninist Communism, let alone the state parties of the Soviet
and Chinese type. None of these as yet existed. 'Party' still meant
essentially a tendency or current of opinion or policy, although Marx
and Engels recognized that once this found expression in class movements, it developed some kind of organization ('diese Organisation der
Proletarier zur Klasse, und damit zur politischen Partei'). Hence the
distinction in Section IV between the 'existing working-class parties ...
the Chartists in England and the agrarian reformers in America' and
the others, not yet so constituted.[8] As the text made clear, at this stage
Marx's and Engels's Communist Party was no kind of organization, nor
did it attempt to establish one – let alone an organization with a specific

---

[8]   The original German begins this section by discussing 'das Verhältniss der
Kommunisten zu den bereits konstituierten Arbeiterparteien ... also den
Chartisten', etc. The official English translation of 1887, revised by Engels,
attenuates the contrast. A more faithful rendition would compare the 'already
constituted workers' parties' such as the Chartists, etc., with those not yet so
constituted.

programme distinct from that of other organizations.[9] Incidentally, nowhere is the actual body on whose behalf the Manifesto was written, the Communist League, mentioned in it.

Moreover, it is clear not only that the Manifesto was written in and for a particular historical situation, but also that it represented one phase – a relatively immature phase – in the development of Marxian thought. This is most evident in its economic aspects. Although Marx had begun to study political economy seriously from 1843 onwards, he did not set out to develop the economic analysis expounded in *Capital* until he arrived in his English exile after the 1848 Revolution, and acquired access to the treasures of the British Museum Library in the summer of 1850. Thus the distinction between the proletarian's sale of his *labour* to the capitalist and the sale of his *labour-power*, which is essential to the Marxian theory of surplus-value and exploitation, had clearly not yet been made in the Manifesto. Nor did the mature Marx hold the view that the price of the commodity 'labour' was its cost of production – that is, the cost of the physiological minimum of keeping the worker alive. In short, Marx wrote the Manifesto less as a Marxian economist than as a communist Ricardian.

And yet, though Marx and Engels reminded readers that the Manifesto was a historical document, out of date in many respects, they promoted and assisted the publication of the 1848 text, with relatively minor amendments and clarifications.[10] They recognized that it

[9]   'The Communists do not form a separate party opposed to other working-class parties.... They do not set up any sectarian principles of their own, by which to shape and mould the proletarian movement' (Section II).

[10] The best-known of these, underlined by Lenin, was the observation, in the 1872 preface, that the Paris Commune had shown 'that the working class cannot simply

remained a major statement of the analysis which distinguished their communism from all other projects for the creation of a better society. In essence this analysis was historical. Its core was the demonstration of the historical development of societies, and specifically of bourgeois society, which replaced its predecessors, revolutionized the world, and in turn necessarily created the conditions for its inevitable supersession. Unlike Marxian economics, the 'materialist conception of history' which underlay this analysis had already found its mature formulation in the mid–1840s, and remained substantially unchanged in later years.[11] In this respect the Manifesto was already a defining document of Marxism. It embodied the historical vision, though its general outline remained to be filled in by fuller analysis.

---

lay hold of the ready-made state machinery, and wield it for its own purposes'. After Marx's death Engels added the footnote modifying the first sentence of Section I to exclude prehistoric societies from the universal scope of class struggle. However, neither Marx nor Engels bothered to comment on or modify the economic passages of the document. Whether Marx and Engels really considered a fuller 'Umarbeitung oder Ergänzung' of the Manifesto (Preface to German edition of 1883) may be doubted, but not that Marx's death made such a rewriting impossible.

[11]   Compare the passage in Section II of the Manifesto ('Does it require deep intuition to comprehend that man's ideas, views and conceptions, in one word, man's consciousness, changes with every change in the conditions of his material existence, in his social relations and in his social life?') with the corresponding passage in the *Preface to the Critique of Political Economy* ('It is not the consciousness of men that determines their existence, but, on the contrary, it is their social existence that determines their consciousness.').

III

How will the Manifesto strike the reader who comes to it today for the first time? The new reader can hardly fail to be swept away by the passionate conviction, the concentrated brevity, the intellectual and stylistic force, of this astonishing pamphlet. It is written, as though in a single creative burst, in lapidary sentences almost naturally transforming themselves into the memorable aphorisms which have become known far beyond the world of political debate: from the opening 'A spectre is haunting Europe – the spectre of Communism' to the final 'The proletarians have nothing to lose but their chains. They have a world to win.'[12] Equally uncommon in nineteenth-century German writing: it is written in short, apodictic paragraphs, mainly of one to five lines – in only five cases, out of more than two hundred, of fifteen or more lines. Whatever else it is, *The Communist Manifesto* as political rhetoric has an almost biblical force. In short, it is impossible to deny its compelling power as literature.[13]

However, what will undoubtedly also strike the contemporary reader is the Manifesto's remarkable diagnosis of the revolutionary character and impact of 'bourgeois society'. The point is not simply that Marx recognized and proclaimed the extraordinary achievements and dynamism

---

[12] Although this is the English version approved by Engels, it is not a strictly correct translation of the original text: 'Mögen die herrschenden Klassen vor einer kommunistischen Revolution zittern. Die Proletarier haben nichts *in ihr* ['in it', i.e. 'in the Revolution'; emphases added] zu verlieren als ihre Ketten.'

[13] For a stylistic analysis, see S.S. Prawer, *Karl Marx and World Literature* (Verso, New York 2011), pp. 148–9. The translations of the Manifesto known to me do not have the literary force of the original German text.

of a society he detested – to the surprise of more than one later defender of capitalism against the red menace. It is that the world transformed by capitalism which he described in 1848, in passages of dark, laconic eloquence, is recognizably the world in which we live 150 years later. Curiously, the politically quite unrealistic optimism of two revolutionaries, twenty-eight and thirty years of age, has proved to be the Manifesto's most lasting strength. For though the 'spectre of Communism' did indeed haunt politicians, and though Europe was living through a major period of economic and social crisis, and was about to erupt in the greatest continent-wide revolution of its history, there were plainly no adequate grounds for the Manifesto's belief that the moment for the overthrow of capitalism was approaching (the bourgeois revolution in Germany will be but the prelude to an immediately following proletarian revolution'). On the contrary. As we now know, capitalism was poised for its first era of triumphant global advance.

Two things give the Manifesto its force. The first is its vision, even at the outset of the triumphal march of capitalism, that this mode of production was not permanent, stable, 'the end of history', but a temporary phase in the history of humanity – one due, like its predecessors, to be superseded by another kind of society (unless – the Manifesto's phrase has not been much noted – it founders 'in the common ruin of the contending classes').The second is its recognition of the necessary *long-term* historical tendencies of capitalist development.The revolutionary potential of the capitalist economy was already evident – Marx and Engels did not claim to be the only ones to recognize it. Since the French Revolution some of the tendencies they observed were plainly having substantial effect – for instance, the decline of 'independent, or but loosely connected provinces, with separate interests, laws, governments and systems of taxation' before nation-states 'with one government, one code of laws, one national class interest, one frontier and one customs tariff'. Nevertheless, by the late 1840s what 'the bourgeoisie' had achieved was a great deal more modest than the miracles ascribed to it in the Manifesto. After all, in 1850 the world produced no more than 71,000 tons of steel (almost 70 per cent of that in Britain) and had built less than 24,000 miles of railroads (two-thirds of these in Britain and the USA). Historians have had no difficulty in showing that even in Britain the Industrial Revolution (a term specifically used by Engels from 1844 on)[14] had hardly created an industrial – or even a predominantly urban – country before the 1850s. Marx and Engels did not describe the world as it had already been transformed by capitalism in 1848; they predicted how it was logically destined to be transformed by it.

Now, in the third millennium of the Western calendar, we live in a world in which this transformation has largely taken place. In some ways we can even see the force of the Manifesto's predictions more clearly than the generations between us and its publication. For until the revolution in transport and communications since the Second World War, there were limits to the globalization of production, to 'giv[ing] a cosmopolitan character to production and consumption in every country'. Until the 1970s industrialization remained overwhelmingly confined to its regions of origin. Some schools of Marxists could even argue that capitalism, at least in its imperialist form, far from 'compel[ling] all nations, on pain of extinction, to adopt the bourgeois mode of production', was by its nature perpetuating – or even creating – 'underdevelopment' in the so-called Third World. While one-third of the human race lived in

[14]   In 'Die Lage Englands. Das 18. Jahrhundert' (Marx–Engels *Werke* I, pp. 566–8).

economies of the Soviet Communist type, it seemed as though capitalism would never succeed in compelling all nations 'to become bourgeois
themselves'. It would not 'create a world after its own image'. Again,
before the 1960s the Manifesto's announcement that capitalism brought
about the destruction of the family seemed not to have been verified,
even in the advanced Western countries where today something like half
of all children are born to or brought up by single mothers, and half of
all households in big cities consist of single persons.

In short, what might in 1848 have struck an uncommitted reader as
revolutionary rhetoric – or, at best, as plausible prediction – can now be
read as a concise characterization of capitalism at the end of the twentieth century. Of what other document of the 1840s can this be said?

IV

However, if at the end of the millennium we must be struck by the acuteness of the Manifesto's vision of the then remote future of a massively
globalized capitalism, the failure of another of its forecasts is equally
striking. It is now evident that the bourgeoisie has not produced 'above all
… its own gravediggers' in the proletariat. 'Its fall and the victory of the
proletariat' have not proved 'equally inevitable'. The contrast between
the two halves of the Manifesto's analysis in its section on 'Bourgeois and
Proletarians' calls for more explanation after 150 years than it did at the
time of its centenary.

The problem lies not in Marx's and Engels's vision of a capitalism
which necessarily transformed most of the people earning their living
in this economy into men and women who depend for their livelihood on hiring themselves out for wages or salaries. It has undoubtedly

tended to do so, though today the incomes of some who are technically employees hired for a salary, such as corporation executives, can hardly count as proletarian. Nor does it lie essentially in their belief that most of this working population would consist of a workforce of *industrial* labour. While Great Britain remained quite exceptional as a country in which wage-paid manual workers formed the absolute majority of the population, the development of industrial production required massive and growing inputs of manual labour for well over a century after the Manifesto. Unquestionably this is no longer the case in modern capital-intensive high-tech production, a development not considered in the Manifesto, though in fact in his more mature economic studies Marx himself envisaged the possible development of an increasingly labour-less economy, at least in a post-capitalist era.[15] Even in the old industrial economies of capitalism, the percentage of people employed in manu-facturing industry remained stable until the 1970s, except for the USA, where the decline set in a little earlier. Indeed, with very few exceptions – such as Britain, Belgium and the USA – in 1970 industrial workers probably formed a larger proportion of the total occupied population in the industrial and industrializing world than ever before.

In any case, the overthrow of capitalism envisaged by the Manifesto relied not on the prior transformation of the *majority* of the occupied population into proletarians but on the assumption that the situation of the proletariat in the capitalist economy was such that, once organized as a necessarily political class movement, it could take the lead in, and rally

---

[15]   See, for example, the discussion of 'Fixed capital and the development of the pro-ductive resources of society' in the 1857–58 manuscripts. *Collected Works*, vol. 29 (1987), pp. 80–99.

round itself, the discontent of other classes, and thus acquire political power as 'the independent movement of the immense majority, in the interest of the immense majority'. Thus the proletariat would 'rise to be the leading class of the nation ... constitute itself as the nation'.[16]

Since capitalism has not been overthrown, we are apt to dismiss this prediction. Yet – utterly improbable though it looked in 1848 – the politics of most European capitalist countries were to be transformed by the rise of organized political movements basing themselves on the class-conscious working class, which had barely made its appearance outside Great Britain. Labour and socialist parties emerged in most parts of the 'developed' world in the 1880s, becoming mass parties in states with the democratic franchise which they did so much to bring about. During and after World War I, as one branch of 'proletarian parties' followed the revolutionary road of the Bolsheviks, another branch became the sustaining pillars of a democratized capitalism. The Bolshevik branch is no longer of much significance in Europe, or parties of this kind have assimilated to social-democracy. Social-Democracy, as understood in the days of Bebel or even Clement Attlee, is fighting a rearguard action. Nevertheless the social-democratic parties of the Second International, sometimes under their original names, are still potentially the parties of government in several European states. Though such governments were less common in the early twenty-first century than they had been in the late twentieth, these parties have shown a unique record of continuity as major political agents over more than a century.

---

[16] The German phrase 'sich zur nationalen Klasse erheben' had Hegelian connotations which the English translation authorized by Engels modified, presumably because he thought it would not be understood by readers in the 1880s.

In short, what is wrong is not the Manifesto's prediction of the central role of the political movements based on the working class (and still sometimes specifically bearing the class name, as in the British, Dutch, Norwegian and Australasian Labour Parties). It is the proposition: 'Of all the classes that stand face to face with the bourgeoisie today, the proletariat alone is a really revolutionary class', whose inevitable destiny, implicit in the nature and development of capitalism, is to overthrow the bourgeoisie: 'Its fall and the victory of the proletariat are equally inevitable.'

Even in the notoriously 'hungry forties', the mechanism which was to ensure this – the inevitable pauperization[17] of the labourers – was not totally convincing; unless on the assumption, implausible even then, that capitalism was in its final crisis and about to be *immediately* overthrown. It was a double mechanism. In addition to the effect of pauperization on the workers' movement, it proved that the bourgeoisie was 'unfit to rule because it is incompetent to assure an existence to its slave within his slavery, because it cannot help letting him sink into such a state that it has to feed him, instead of being fed by him'. Far from providing the profit which fuelled the engine of capitalism, labour now drained it away. But – given the enormous economic potential of capitalism so dramatically expounded in the Manifesto itself – why was it inevitable that capitalism could not provide a livelihood, however miserable, for most of its working class or, alternatively, that it could

---

[17] Pauperism should not be read as a synonym for 'poverty'. The German words, borrowed from English usage, are 'Pauper' ('a destitute person ... one supported by charity or by some public provision': *Chambers' Twentieth Century Dictionary*) and 'Pauperismus' (pauperism: 'state of being a pauper': ibid.).

not afford a welfare system? That 'pauperism [in the strict sense; see Note 17] develops even more rapidly than population and wealth'?[18] If capitalism had a long life before it as became obvious very soon after 1848 this did not have to happen, and indeed it did not.

The Manifesto's vision of the historic development of 'bourgeois society', including the working class which it generated, did not *necessarily* lead to the conclusion that the proletariat would overthrow capitalism and, in so doing, open the way to the development of communism, because vision and conclusion did not derive from the same analysis. The aim of communism, adopted before Marx became 'Marxist', was derived not from the analysis of the nature and development of capitalism but from a philosophical – indeed, an eschatological – argument about human nature and destiny. The idea – fundamental for Marx from then on – that the proletariat was a class which could not liberate itself without thereby liberating society as a whole first appears as 'a philosophical deduction rather than a product of observation'.[19] As George Lichtheim put it: 'the proletariat makes its first appearance in Marx' writings as the social force needed to realise the aims of German philosophy' as Marx saw it in 1843–44.[20]

---

[18]   Paradoxically, something like the Marxian argument of 1848 is widely used today by capitalists and free-market governments to prove that the economies of states whose GNP continues to double every few decades will be bankrupted if they do not abolish the systems of income transfer (welfare states, etc.), installed in poorer times, by which those who earn maintain those who are unable to earn.

[19]   Leszek Kolakowski, *Main Currents of Marxism*, vol. 1, *The Founders* (Oxford 1978), p. 130.

[20]   George Lichtheim, *Marxism* (London 1964), p. 45.

The '*positive* possibility of German emancipation', wrote Marx in the *Introduction to a Critique of Hegel's Philosophy of Law*, lay:

in the formation of a class with *radical chains* ... a class which is the dissolution of all classes, a sphere of society which has a universal character because its sufferings are universal, and which claims no *particular right* because the wrong committed against it is not a *particular wrong*, but wrong *as such*.... This dissolution of society as a particular class is the *proletariat*.... The emancipation of the German is the emancipation of *the human being*. *Philosophy* is the *head* of this emancipation and the *proletariat* is its *heart*. Philosophy cannot realise itself without abolishing the proletariat, and the proletariat cannot be abolished without philosophy being made a reality.[21]

At this time Marx knew little more about the proletariat than that 'it is coming into being in Germany only as a result of the rising industrial development', and this was precisely its potential as a liberating force, since, unlike the poor masses of traditional society, it was the child of 'a *drastic dissolution* of society', and therefore by its existence 'proclaim[ed] the *dissolution of the hitherto existing world order*'. He knew even less about labour movements, though he knew a great deal about the history of the French Revolution. In Engels he acquired a partner who brought to the partnership the concept of the 'Industrial Revolution', an understanding of the dynamics of capitalist economy as it actually existed in Britain, and

---

[21] *Collected Works*, vol. 3 (1975), pp. 186–7. In this passage I have generally preferred the translation in Lichtheim, *Marxism*. The German word translated by him as 'class' is 'Stand', which is misleading today.

the rudiments of an economic analysis,[22] all of which led him to predict a future social revolution, to be fomented by an actual working class about which, living and working in Britain in the early 1840s, he knew a great deal. Marx's and Engels's approaches to 'the proletariat' and communism complemented one another. So did their respective conceptions of the class struggle as a motor of history – in Marx's case derived largely from the study of the French Revolutionary period; in Engels's from the experience of social movements in post-Napoleonic Britain. It is no surprise that they found themselves (in Engels's words) 'in agreement in all theoretical fields'.[23] Engels brought to Marx the elements of a model which demonstrated the fluctuating and self-destabilizing nature of the operations of the capitalist economy – notably the outlines of a theory of economic crises[24] – and empirical material about the rise of the British working-class movement and the revolutionary role it could play in Britain.

In the 1840s the conclusion that society was on the verge of revolution was not implausible. Nor was the prediction that the working class, however immature, would lead it. After all, within weeks of the publication of the Manifesto a movement of the Paris workers overthrew the French monarchy, and gave the signal for revolution to half of Europe. Nevertheless, the tendency for capitalist development to generate

---

[22]   Published as *Outlines of a Critique of Political Economy* in 1844 (*Collected Works*, vol. 3, pp. 418–43).

[23]   'On the History of the Communist League' (*Collected Works*, vol. 26, 1990), p. 318.

[24]   'Outlines of a Critique' (*CollectedWorks*, vol. 3, pp. 433 ff). This seems to have been derived from radical British writers, notably John Wade, *History of the Middle and Working Classes* (London 1835), to whom Engels refers in this connection.

an essentially *revolutionary* proletariat could not be deduced from the analysis of the nature of capitalist development. It was one possible consequence of this development, but could not be shown to be the only possible one. Still less could it be shown that a successful overthrow of capitalism by the proletariat must necessarily open the way to communist development. (The Manifesto claims no more than that it would then initiate a process of very gradual change.)[25] Marx's vision of a proletariat whose very essence destined it to emancipate all humanity, and end class society by its overthrow of capitalism, represents a hope read into his analysis of capitalism, but not a conclusion necessarily imposed by that analysis.

What the Manifesto's analysis of capitalism could undoubtedly lead to – especially when it is extended by Marx's analysis of economic concentration, which is barely hinted at in 1848 – is a more general and less specific conclusion about the self-destructive forces built into capitalist development. It must reach a point – and in 2012 it is not only Marxists who will accept this – where:

Modern bourgeois society with its relations of production, of exchange and of property, a society that has conjured up such gigantic means of production and of exchange, is like the sorcerer who is no longer able to control the powers of the nether world, whom he has called up.... The conditions of bourgeois society arc too narrow to encompass the wealth created by them.

[25] This is even clearer from Engels's formulations in what are, in effect, two preliminary drafts of the Manifesto, 'Draft of a Communist Confession of Faith' (*Collected Works*, vol. 6, p. 102) and 'Principles of Communism' (ibid., p. 350).

It is not unreasonable to conclude that the 'contradictions' inherent in a market system based on 'no other nexus between man and man than naked self-interest, than callous "cash payment"', a system of exploitation and of 'endless accumulation' can never be overcome; that at some point in a series of transformations and restructurings the development of this essentially self-destabilizing system will lead to a state of affairs that can no longer be described as capitalism. Or – to quote the later Marx – when 'centralisation of the means of production and the socialisation of labour at last reach a point where they become incompatible with their capitalist integument', and that 'integument is burst asunder'.[26] By what name the subsequent state of affairs is described is immaterial. However – as the effects of the world economic explosion on the world environment demonstrate – it will necessarily have to mark a sharp shift away from private appropriation to social management on a global scale.

It is extremely unlikely that such a 'post-capitalist society' would correspond to the traditional models of socialism, and still less to the 'really existing' socialisms of the Soviet era. What forms it might take, and how far it would embody the humanist values of Marx's and Engels's communism, would depend on the political action through which this change came about. For this, as the Manifesto holds, is central to the shaping of historical change.

[26]   From 'Historical Tendency of Capitalist Accumulation', in *Capital*, vol. I (*Collected Works*, vol. 35, 1996), p. 750.

V

In the Marxian view, however we describe that historic moment when 'the integument is burst asunder', politics will be an essential element in it. The Manifesto has been read primarily as a document of historical inevitability, and indeed its force derived largely from the confidence it gave its readers that capitalism was inevitably destined to be buried by its gravediggers, and that now – and at no earlier era in history – the conditions for emancipation had come into being. Yet contrary to widespread assumptions – inasmuch as it believes that historical change proceeds through men making their own history, it is not a determinist document. The graves have to be dug by or through human action.

A determinist reading of the argument is indeed possible. It has been suggested that Engels tended towards it more naturally than Marx, with important consequences for the development of Marxist theory and the Marxist labour movement after Marx's death. However, though Engels's own earlier drafts have been cited as evidence,[27] it cannot in fact be read into the Manifesto itself. When it leaves the field of historical analysis and enters the present, it is a document of choices, of political possibilities rather than probabilities, let alone certainties. Between 'now' and the unpredictable time when, 'in the course of development', there would be 'an association, in which the free development of each is the condition for the free development of all' lies the realm of political action.

Historical change through social praxis, through collective action, is at its core. The Manifesto sees the development of the proletariat as the 'organization of the proletarians into a class, and consequently into a

---

[27] Lichtheim, *Marxism*, pp. 58–60.

political party'. The 'conquest of political power by the proletariat' (the winning of democracy') is 'the first step in the workers' revolution', and the future of society hinges on the subsequent political actions of the new regime (how 'the proletariat will use its political supremacy'). The commitment to *politics* is what, historically, distinguished Marxian socialism from the anarchists, and the successors of those socialists whose rejection of all political action the Manifesto specifically condemns. Even before Lenin, Marxian theory was not just about 'what history shows us will happen', but also about 'what must be done'. Admittedly, the twentieth-century Soviet experience has taught us that it might be better not to do 'what must be done' under historical conditions which virtually put success beyond reach. But this lesson might also have been learned from considering the implications of *The Communist Manifesto*.

But then, the Manifesto – and this is not the least of its remarkable qualities – is a document which envisaged failure. It hoped that the outcome of capitalist development would be 'A revolutionary reconstitution of society at large' but, as we have already seen, it did not exclude the alternative: 'common ruin'. Many years later, another Marxian rephrased this as the choice between socialism and barbarity. Which of these will prevail is a question which the twenty-first century must be left to answer.

MANIFESTO OF THE COMMUNIST PARTY

Karl Marx and Frederick Engels

A spectre is haunting Europe – the spectre of Communism. All the powers of old Europe have entered into a holy alliance to exorcize this spectre: Pope and Tsar, Metternich[1] and Guizot,[2] French radicals and German police spies.

Where is the party in opposition that has not been decried as communistic by its opponents in power? Where the opposition that has not hurled back the branding reproach of Communism, against the more advanced opposition parties, as well as against its reactionary adversaries?

Two things result from this fact:

1. Communism is already acknowledged by all European powers to be itself a power.

---

[1] Clemens Lothar, Prince Metternich, was the leading Austrian statesman from 1809 to 1848 and the architect of the counter-revolutionary Holy Alliance.

[2] François Guizot was a French historian and *de facto* Prime Minister from 1840 to 1848 under the Orleanist 'July' monarchy of Louis Philippe.

2.   It is high time that Communists should openly, in the face of the whole world, publish their views, their aims, their tendencies, and meet this nursery tale of the Spectre of Communism with a manifesto of the party itself.

To this end, Communists of various nationalities have assembled in London, and sketched the following manifesto, to be published in the English, French, German, Italian, Flemish and Danish languages.

1. Bourgeois and Proletarians[3]

The history of all hitherto existing society[4] is the history of class struggles.

---

[3]   By bourgeoisie is meant the class of modern capitalists, owners of the means of social production and employers of wage labour. By proletariat, the class of modern wage labourers who, having no means of production of their own, are reduced to selling their labour power in order to live [Engels].

[4]   That is, all *written* history. In 1847, the pre-history of society, the social organization existing previous to recorded history, was all but unknown. Since then, Haxthausen discovered common ownership of land in Russia, Maurer proved it to be the social foundation from which all Teutonic races started in history, and by and by village communities were found to be, or to have been the primitive form of society everywhere from India to Ireland. The inner organization of this primitive communistic society was laid bare, in its typical form, by Morgan's crowning discovery of the true nature of the *gens* and its relation to the *tribe*. With the dissolution of these primeval communities society begins to be differentiated into separate and finally antagonistic classes. I have attempted to retrace this process of dissolution in: *Der Ursprung der Familie, des Privateigenthums und des Staats* (*The Origin of the Family, Private Property and the State*) [Engels].

Freeman and slave, patrician and plebeian, lord and serf, guild-master[5] and journeyman, in a word, oppressor and oppressed, stood in constant opposition to one another, carried on an uninterrupted, now hidden, now open fight, a fight that each time ended, either in a revolutionary reconstitution of society at large, or in the common ruin of the contending classes.

In the earlier epochs of history, we find almost everywhere a complicated arrangement of society into various orders, a manifold gradation of social rank. In ancient Rome we have patricians, knights, plebeians, slaves; in the Middle Ages, feudal lords, vassals, guild-masters, journeymen, apprentices, serfs; in almost all of these classes, again, subordinate gradations.

The modern bourgeois society that has sprouted from the ruins of feudal society has not done away with class antagonisms. It has but established new classes, new conditions of oppression, new forms of struggle in place of the old ones.

Our epoch, the epoch of the bourgeoisie, possesses, however, this distinctive feature: it has simplified the class antagonisms. Society as a whole is more and more splitting up into two great hostile camps, into two great classes directly facing each other: bourgeoisie and proletariat.

From the serfs of the Middle Ages sprang the chartered burghers of the earliest towns. From these burgesses the first elements of the bourgeoisie were developed.

The discovery of America, the rounding of the Cape, opened up fresh ground for the rising bourgeoisie. The East Indian and Chinese

---

[5] Guild-master, that is, a full member of a guild, a master within, not a head of a guild [Engels].

markets, the colonization of America, trade with the colonies, the increase in the means of exchange and in commodities generally, gave to commerce, to navigation, to industry, an impulse never before known, and thereby, to the revolutionary element in the tottering feudal society, a rapid development.

The feudal system of industry, under which industrial production was monopolized by closed guilds, now no longer sufficed for the growing wants of the new markets. The manufacturing system took its place. The guild-masters were pushed on one side by the manufacturing middle class; division of labour between the different corporate guilds vanished in the face of division of labour in each single workshop.

Meantime the markets kept ever growing, the demand ever rising. Even manufacture no longer sufficed. Thereupon, steam and machinery revolutionized industrial production. The place of manufacture was taken by the giant, modern industry, the place of the industrial middle class, by industrial millionaires, the leaders of whole industrial armies, the modern bourgeois.

Modern industry has established the world market, for which the discovery of America paved the way. This market has given an immense development to commerce, to navigation, to communication by land. This development has, in its turn, reacted on the extension of industry; and in proportion as industry, commerce, navigation, railways extended, in the same proportion the bourgeoisie developed, increased its capital, and pushed into the background every class handed down from the Middle Ages.

We see, therefore, how the modern bourgeoisie is itself the product of a long course of development, of a series of revolutions in the modes of production and of exchange.

Each step in the development of the bourgeoisie was accompanied by a corresponding political advance of that class. An oppressed class under the sway of the feudal nobility, an armed and self-governing association in the medieval commune;[6] here independent urban republic (as in Italy and Germany), there taxable 'third estate' of the monarchy (as in France), afterwards, in the period of manufacture proper, serving either the semi-feudal or the absolute monarchy as a counterpoise against the nobility, and, in fact, corner-stone of the great monarchies in general, the bourgeoisie has at last, since the establishment of modern industry and of the world market, conquered for itself, in the modern representative state, exclusive political sway. The executive of the modern state is but a committee for managing the common affairs of the whole bourgeoisie.

The bourgeoisie, historically, has played a most revolutionary part.

The bourgeoisie, wherever it has got the upper hand, has put an end to all feudal, patriarchal, idyllic relations. It has pitilessly torn asunder the motley feudal ties that bound man to his 'natural superiors', and has left remaining no other nexus between man and man than naked self-interest, than callous 'cash payment'. It has drowned the most heavenly ecstasies of religious fervour, of chivalrous enthusiasm, of philistine sentimentalism, in the icy water of egotistical calculation. It has resolved personal worth into exchange value, and in place of the numberless

---

[6] 'Commune' was the name taken, in France, by the nascent towns even before they had conquered, from their feudal lords and masters, local self-government and political rights as the 'third estate'. Generally speaking, for the economic development of the bourgeoisie, England is here taken as the typical country; for its political development, France [Engels].

indefeasible chartered freedoms, has set up that single, unconscionable freedom – free trade. In one word, for exploitation, veiled by religious and political illusions, it has substituted naked, shameless, direct, brutal exploitation.

The bourgeoisie has stripped of its halo every occupation hitherto honoured and looked up to with reverent awe. It has converted the physician, the lawyer, the priest, the poet, the man of science, into its paid wage labourers.

The bourgeoisie has torn away from the family its sentimental veil, and has reduced the family relation to a mere money relation.

The bourgeoisie has disclosed how it came to pass that the brutal display of vigour in the Middle Ages, which reactionists so much admire, found its fitting complement in the most slothful indolence. It has been the first to show what man's activity can bring about. It has accomplished wonders far surpassing Egyptian pyramids, Roman aqueducts, and Gothic cathedrals; it has conducted expeditions that put in the shade all former exoduses of nations and crusades.

The bourgeoisie cannot exist without constantly revolutionizing the instruments of production, and thereby the relations of production, and with them the whole relations of society. Conservation of the old modes of production in unaltered form, was, on the contrary, the first condition of existence for all earlier industrial classes. Constant revolutionizing of production, uninterrupted disturbance of all social conditions, everlasting uncertainty and agitation distinguish the bourgeois epoch from all earlier ones. All fixed, fast-frozen relations, with their train of ancient and venerable prejudices and opinions, are swept away, all new-formed ones become antiquated before they can ossify. All that is solid melts into air, all that is holy is profaned, and man is at last compelled to face with sober senses, his real conditions of life, and his relations with his kind.

The need of a constantly expanding market for its products chases the bourgeoisie over the whole surface of the globe. It must nestle everywhere, settle everywhere, establish connections everywhere.

The bourgeoisie has through its exploitation of the world market given a cosmopolitan character to production and consumption in every country. To the great chagrin of reactionists, it has drawn from under the feet of industry the national ground on which it stood. All old-established national industries have been destroyed or are daily being destroyed. They are dislodged by new industries, whose introduction becomes a life and death question for all civilized nations, by industries that no longer work up indigenous raw material, but raw material drawn from the remotest zones; industries whose products are consumed, not only at home, but in every quarter of the globe. In place of the old wants, satisfied by the productions of the country, we find new wants, requiring for their satisfaction the products of distant lands and climes. In place of the old local and national seclusion and self-sufficiency, we have intercourse in every direction, universal interdependence of nations. And as in material, so also in intellectual production. The intellectual creations of individual nations become common property. National one-sidedness and narrow-mindedness become more and more impossible, and from the numerous national and local literatures, there arises a world literature.

The bourgeoisie, by the rapid improvement of all instruments of production, by the immensely facilitated means of communication, draws all, even the most barbarian, nations into civilization. The cheap prices of its commodities are the heavy artillery with which it batters down all

Chinese walls, with which it forces the barbarians' intensely obstinate hatred of foreigners to capitulate. It compels all nations, on pain of extinction, to adopt the bourgeois mode of production; it compels them to introduce what it calls civilization into their midst, i.e., to become bourgeois themselves. In one word, it creates a world after its own image.

The bourgeoisie has subjected the country to the rule of the towns. It has created enormous cities, has greatly increased the urban population as compared with the rural, and has thus rescued a considerable part of the population from the idiocy of rural life. Just as it has made the country dependent on the towns, so it has made barbarian and semi-barbarian countries dependent on the civilized ones, nations of peasants on nations of bourgeois, the East on the West.

The bourgeoisie keeps more and more doing away with the scattered state of the population, of the means of production, and of property. It has agglomerated population, centralized means of production, and has concentrated property in a few hands. The necessary consequence of this was political centralization. Independent, or but loosely connected provinces, with separate interests, laws, governments and systems of taxation, became lumped together into one nation, with one government, one code of laws, one national class interest, one frontier and one customs tariff.

The bourgeoisie, during its rule of scarce one hundred years, has created more massive and more colossal productive forces than have all preceding generations together. Subjection of nature's forces to man, machinery, application of chemistry to industry and agriculture, steam navigation, railways, electric telegraphs, clearing of whole continents for cultivation, canalization of rivers, whole populations conjured out of the ground – what earlier century had even a presentiment that such productive forces slumbered in the lap of social labour?

We see then: the means of production and of exchange, on whose foundation the bourgeoisie built itself up, were generated in feudal society. At a certain stage in the development of these means of production and of exchange, the conditions under which feudal society produced and exchanged, the feudal organization of agriculture and manufacturing industry, in one word, the feudal relations of property became no longer compatible with the already developed productive forces; they became so many fetters. They had to be burst asunder; they were burst asunder.

Into their place stepped free competition, accompanied by a social and political constitution adapted to it, and by the economical and political sway of the bourgeois class.

A similar movement is going on before our own eyes. Modern bourgeois society with its relations of production, of exchange and of property, a society that has conjured up such gigantic means of production and of exchange, is like the sorcerer, who is no longer able to control the powers of the nether world whom he has called up by his spells. For many a decade past, the history of industry and commerce is but the history of the revolt of modern productive forces against modern conditions of production, against the property relations that are the conditions for the existence of the bourgeoisie and of its rule. It is enough to mention the commercial crises that by their periodical return put on trial, each time more threateningly, the existence of the entire bourgeois society. In these crises a great part not only of the existing products, but also of the previously created productive forces, are periodically destroyed. In these crises there breaks out an epidemic that, in all earlier epochs, would have seemed an absurdity – the epidemic of overproduc-tion. Society suddenly finds itself put back into a state of momentary barbarism; it appears as if a famine, a universal war of devastation had cut off the supply of every means of subsistence; industry and commerce seem to be destroyed; and why? Because there is too much civilization, too much means of subsistence, too much industry, too much com-merce. The productive forces at the disposal of society no longer tend to further the development of the conditions of bourgeois property; on the contrary, they have become too powerful for these conditions, by which they are fettered, and so soon as they overcome these fetters, they bring disorder into the whole of bourgeois society, endanger the existence of bourgeois property. The conditions of bourgeois society are too narrow to comprise the wealth created by them. And how does the bourgeoisie get over these crises? On the one hand by enforced destruction of a mass of productive forces; on the other, by the conquest of new markets, and by the more thorough exploitation of the old ones. That is to say, by paving the way for more extensive and more destructive crises, and by diminishing the means whereby crises are prevented.

The weapons with which the bourgeoisie felled feudalism to the ground are now turned against the bourgeoisie itself.

But not only has the bourgeoisie forged the weapons that bring death to itself; it has also called into existence the men who are to wield those weapons – the modern working class – the proletarians.

In proportion as the bourgeoisie, i.e., capital, is developed, in the same proportion is the proletariat, the modern working class, devel-oped – a class of labourers, who live only so long as they find work, and who find work only so long as their labour increases capital. These labourers, who must sell themselves piecemeal, are a commodity, like every other article of commerce, and are consequently exposed to all the vicissitudes of competition, to all the fluctuations of the market.

Owing to the extensive use of machinery and to division of labour, the work of the proletarians has lost all individual character, and, consequently, all charm for the workman. He becomes an appendage of the machine, and it is only the most simple, most monotonous, and most easily acquired knack, that is required of him. Hence, the cost of production of a workman is restricted, almost entirely, to the means of subsistence that he requires for his maintenance, and for the propagation of his race. But the price of a commodity, and therefore also of labour,[7] is equal to its cost of production. In proportion, therefore, as the repulsiveness of the work increases, the wage decreases. Nay more, in proportion as the use of machinery and division of labour increases, in the same proportion the burden of toil also increases, whether by prolongation of the working hours, by increase of the work exacted in a given time or by increased speed of the machinery, etc.

Modern industry has converted the little workshop of the patriarchal master into the great factory of the industrial capitalist. Masses of labourers, crowded into the factory, are organized like soldiers. As privates of the industrial army they are placed under the command of a perfect hierarchy of officers and sergeants. Not only are they slaves of the bourgeois class, and of the bourgeois state; they are daily and hourly enslaved by the machine, by the overseer, and, above all, by the individual bourgeois

---

[7] In Marx's later theory of surplus value, he concluded that it is the worker's *labour power*, not his labour, that is sold to the capitalist as a commodity. See 'Wages, Prices and Profit', in Marx–Engels, *Selected Works*, Lawrence & Wishart (London 1968).

manufacturer himself. The more openly this despotism proclaims gain to be its end and aim, the more petty, the more hateful and the more embittering it is.

The less the skill and exertion of strength implied in manual labour, in other words, the more modern industry becomes developed, the more is the labour of men superseded by that of women. Differences of age and sex have no longer any distinctive social validity for the working class. All are instruments of labour, more or less expensive to use, according to their age and sex.

No sooner is the exploitation of the labourer by the manufacturer so far at an end that he receives his wages in cash, than he is set upon by the other portions of the bourgeoisie, the landlord, the shopkeeper, the pawnbroker, etc.

The lower strata of the middle class – the small tradespeople, shop-keepers, and *rentiers*, the handicraftsmen and peasants – all these sink gradually into the proletariat, partly because their diminutive capital does not suffice for the scale on which modern industry is carried on, and is swamped in the competition with the large capitalists, partly because their specialized skill is rendered worthless by new methods of production. Thus the proletariat is recruited from all classes of the population.

The proletariat goes through various stages of development. With its birth begins its struggle with the bourgeoisie. At first the contest is carried on by individual labourers, then by the workpeople of a fac-tory, then by the operatives of one trade, in one locality, against the individual bourgeois who directly exploits them. They direct their attacks not against the bourgeois conditions of production, but against the instruments of production themselves; they destroy imported wares that compete with their labour, they smash to pieces machinery, they set factories ablaze, they seek to restore by force the vanished status of the workman of the Middle Ages.

At this stage the labourers still form an incoherent mass scattered over the whole country, and broken up by their mutual competition. If anywhere they unite to form more compact bodies, this is not yet the consequence of their own active union, but of the union of the bourgeoisie, which class, in order to attain its own political ends, is compelled to set the whole proletariat in motion, and is moreover yet, for a time, able to do so. At this stage, therefore, the proletarians do not fight their enemies, but the enemies of their enemies, the remnants of absolute monarchy, the landowners, the non-industrial bourgeois, the petty bourgeoisie. Thus the whole historical movement is concentrated in the hands of the bourgeoisie; every victory so obtained is a victory for the bourgeoisie.

But with the development of industry the proletariat not only increases in number; it becomes concentrated in greater masses, its strength grows, and it feels that strength more. The various interests and conditions of life within the ranks of the proletariat are more and more equalized, in proportion as machinery obliterates all distinctions of labour, and nearly everywhere reduces wages to the same low level. The growing competition among the bourgeois, and the resulting commercial crises, make the wages of the workers ever more fluctuating. The unceasing improvement of machinery, ever more rapidly developing, makes their livelihood more and more precarious; the collisions between individual workmen and individual bourgeois take more and more the character of collisions between two classes. Thereupon the workers begin to form combinations (trade unions) against the bourgeois; they club together in order to keep up the rate of wages; they found permanent associations in order to make provision beforehand for these occasional revolts. Here and there the contest breaks out into riots.

Now and then the workers are victorious, but only for a time. The real fruit of their battles lies, not in the immediate result, but in the ever expanding union of the workers. This union is helped on by the improved means of communication that are created by modern industry, and that place the workers of different localities in contact with one another. It was just this contact that was needed to centralize the numerous local struggles, all of the same character, into one national struggle between classes. But every class struggle is a political struggle. And that union, to attain which the burghers of the Middle Ages, with their miserable highways, required centuries, the modern proletarians, thanks to railways, achieve in a few years.

This organization of the proletarians into a class, and consequently into a political party, is continually being upset again by the competition between the workers themselves. But it ever rises up again, stronger, firmer, mightier. It compels legislative recognition of particular interests of the workers, by taking advantage of the divisions among the bourgeoisie itself. Thus the Ten Hours Bill in England was carried.[8]

Altogether, collisions between the classes of the old society further, in many ways, the course of development of the proletariat. The bourgeoisie finds itself involved in a constant battle: at first with the aristocracy; later on, with those portions of the bourgeoisie itself, whose

---

[8]   In 1846. See Engels's article 'The English Ten Hours Bill', Marx–Engels, *Articles on Britain*, Progress Publishers (Moscow 1971), pp. 96–108.

interests have become antagonistic to the progress of industry; at all times, with the bourgeoisie of foreign countries. In all these battles it sees itself compelled to appeal to the proletariat, to ask for its help, and thus to drag it into the political arena. The bourgeoisie itself, therefore, supplies the proletariat with its own elements of political and general education, in other words, it furnishes the proletariat with weapons for fighting the bourgeoisie.

Further, as we have already seen, entire sections of the ruling classes are, by the advance of industry, precipitated into the proletariat, or are at least threatened in their conditions of existence. These also supply the proletariat with fresh elements of enlightenment and progress.

Finally, in times when the class struggle nears the decisive hour, the process of dissolution going on within the ruling class, in fact within the whole range of old society, assumes such a violent, glaring character, that a small section of the ruling class cuts itself adrift, and joins the revolutionary class, the class that holds the future in its hands. Just as, therefore, at an earlier period, a section of the nobility went over to the bourgeoisie, so now a portion of the bourgeoisie goes over to the proletariat, and in particular, a portion of the bourgeois ideologists, who have raised themselves to the level of comprehending theoretically the historical movement as a whole.

Of all the classes that stand face to face with the bourgeoisie today, the proletariat alone is a really revolutionary class. The other classes decay and finally disappear in the face of modern industry; the proletariat is its special and essential product.

The lower middle class, the small manufacturer, the shopkeeper, the artisan, the peasant, all these fight against the bourgeoisie, to save from extinction their existence as fractions of the middle class. They are therefore not revolutionary, but conservative. Nay more, they are reactionary, for they try to roll back the wheel of history. If by chance they are revolutionary, they are so only in view of their impending transfer into the proletariat, they thus defend not their present, but their future interests, they desert their own standpoint to place themselves at that of the proletariat.

The 'dangerous class',[9] the social scum, that passively rotting mass thrown off by the lowest layers of old society, may, here and there, be swept into the movement by a proletarian revolution; its conditions of life, however, prepare it far more for the part of a bribed tool of reactionary intrigue.

In the conditions of the proletariat, those of old society at large are already virtually swamped. The proletarian is without property; his relation to his wife and children has no longer anything in common with the bourgeois family relations; modern industrial labour, modern subjection to capital, the same in England as in France, in America as in Germany, has stripped him of every trace of national character. Law, morality, religion, are to him so many bourgeois prejudices, behind which lurk in ambush just as many bourgeois interests.

All the preceding classes that got the upper hand, sought to fortify their already acquired status by subjecting society at large to their conditions of appropriation. The proletarians cannot become masters of the productive forces of society, except by abolishing their own previous mode of appropriation, and thereby also every other previous mode of appropriation. They have nothing of their own to secure and to fortify;

---

[9]   i.e. the lumpenproletariat of casual labourers and unemployed, which was very extensive in the cities of nineteenth-century Europe.

their mission is to destroy all previous securities for, and insurances of, individual property.

All previous historical movements were movements of minorities, or in the interest of minorities. The proletarian movement is the self-conscious, independent movement of the immense majority, in the interest of the immense majority. The proletariat, the lowest stratum of our present society, cannot stir, cannot raise itself up, without the whole superincumbent strata of official society being sprung into the air.

Though not in substance, yet in form, the struggle of the proletariat with the bourgeoisie is at first a national struggle. The proletariat of each country must, of course, first of all settle matters with its own bourgeoisie.

In depicting the most general phases of the development of the proletariat, we traced the more or less veiled civil war, raging within existing society, up to the point where that war breaks out into open revolution, and where the violent overthrow of the bourgeoisie lays the foundation for the sway of the proletariat.

Hitherto, every form of society has been based, as we have already seen, on the antagonism of oppressing and oppressed classes. But in order to oppress a class, certain conditions must be assured to it under which it can, at least, continue its slavish existence. The serf, in the period of serfdom, raised himself to membership in the commune, just as the petty bourgeois, under the yoke of feudal absolutism, managed to develop into a bourgeois. The modern labourer, on the contrary, instead of rising with the progress of industry, sinks deeper and deeper below the conditions of existence of his own class. He becomes a pauper, and pauperism develops more rapidly than population and wealth. And here it becomes evident that the bourgeoisie is unfit any longer to be the ruling class in society, and to impose its conditions of existence upon society as an overriding law. It is unfit to rule because it is incompetent to assure an existence to its slave within his slavery, because it cannot help letting him sink into such a state that it has to feed him, instead of being fed by him. Society can no longer live under this bourgeoisie, in other words, its existence is no longer compatible with society.

The essential condition for the existence, and for the sway of the bourgeois class, is the formation and augmentation of capital; the condition for capital is wage labour. Wage labour rests exclusively on competition between the labourers. The advance of industry, whose involuntary promoter is the bourgeoisie, replaces the isolation of the labourers, due to competition, by their revolutionary combination, due to association. The development of modern industry, therefore, cuts from under its feet the very foundation on which the bourgeoisie produces and appropriates products. What the bourgeoisie therefore produces, above all, are its own grave-diggers. Its fall and the victory of the proletariat are equally inevitable.

II. Proletarians and Communists

In what relation do the Communists stand to the proletarians as a whole?

The Communists do not form a separate party opposed to other working-class parties.

They have no interests separate and apart from those of the proletariat as a whole.

They do not set up any sectarian principles of their own, by which to shape and mould the proletarian movement.

The Communists are distinguished from the other working-class parties by this only:

1. In the national struggles of the proletarians of the different countries, they point out and bring to the front the common interests of the entire proletariat, independently of all nationality.
2. In the various stages of development which the struggle of the working class against the bourgeoisie has to pass through, they always and everywhere represent the interests of the movement as a whole.

The Communists, therefore, are on the one hand, practically, the most advanced and resolute section of the working-class parties of every country, that section which pushes forward all others; on the other hand, theoretically, they have over the great mass of the proletariat the advantage of clearly understanding the line of march, the conditions, and the ultimate general results of the proletarian movement.

The immediate aim of the Communists is the same as that of all the other proletarian parties: formation of the proletariat into a class, overthrow of the bourgeois supremacy, conquest of political power by the proletariat.

The theoretical conclusions of the Communists are in no way based on ideas or principles that have been invented, or discovered, by this or that would-be universal reformer.

They merely express, in general terms, actual relations springing from an existing class struggle, from a historical movement going on under our very eyes. The abolition of existing property relations is not at all a distinctive feature of communism.

All property relations in the past have continually been subject to historical change consequent upon the change in historical conditions.

The French Revolution, for example, abolished feudal property in favour of bourgeois property.

The distinguishing feature of communism is not the abolition of property generally, but the abolition of bourgeois property. But modern bourgeois private property is the final and most complete expression of the system of producing and appropriating products that is based on class antagonisms, on the exploitation of the many by the few.

In this sense, the theory of the Communists may be summed up in the single sentence: Abolition of private property.

We Communists have been reproached with the desire of abolishing the right of personally acquiring property as the fruit of a man's own labour, which property is alleged to be the ground work of all personal freedom, activity and independence.

Hard-won, self-acquired, self-earned property! Do you mean the property of the petty artisan and of the small peasant, a form of property that preceded the bourgeois form? There is no need to abolish that; the development of industry has to a great extent already destroyed it, and is still destroying it daily.

Or do you mean modern bourgeois private property?

But does wage labour create any property for the labourer? Not a bit. It creates capital, i.e., that kind of property which exploits wage labour, and which cannot increase except upon conditions of begetting a new supply of wage labour for fresh exploitation. Property, in its present form, is based on the antagonism of capital and wage labour. Let us examine both sides of this antagonism.

To be a capitalist, is to have not only a purely personal, but a social status in production. Capital is a collective product, and only by the united action of many members, nay, in the last resort, only by the united action of all members of society, can it be set in motion.

Capital is, therefore, not a personal, it is a social power.

When, therefore, capital is converted into common property, into the property of all members of society, personal property is not thereby transformed into social property. It is only the social character of the property that is changed. It loses its class character.

Let us now take wage labour.

The average price of wage labour is the minimum wage, i.e., that quantum of the means of subsistence which is absolutely requisite to keep the labourer in bare existence as a labourer. What, therefore, the wage labourer appropriates by means of his labour, merely suffices to prolong and reproduce a bare existence. We by no means intend to abolish this personal appropriation of the products of labour, an appropriation that is made for the maintenance and reproduction of human life, and that leaves no surplus wherewith to command the labour of others. All that we want to do away with, is the miserable character of this appropriation, under which the labourer lives merely to increase capital, and is allowed to live only in so far as the interest of the ruling class requires it.

In bourgeois society, living labour is but a means to increase accumulated labour. In communist society, accumulated labour is but a means to widen, to enrich, to promote the existence of the labourer.

In bourgeois society, therefore, the past dominates the present; in communist society, the present dominates the past. In bourgeois society capital is independent and has individuality, while the living person is dependent and has no individuality.

And the abolition of this state of things is called by the bourgeois, abolition of individuality and freedom! And rightly so. The abolition of bourgeois individuality, bourgeois independence, and bourgeois freedom is undoubtedly aimed at.

By freedom is meant, under the present bourgeois conditions of production, free trade, free selling and buying.

But if selling and buying disappears, free selling and buying disappears also. This talk about free selling and buying, and all the other 'brave words' of our bourgeoisie about freedom in general, have a meaning, if any, only in contrast with restricted selling and buying, with the fettered traders of the Middle Ages, but have no meaning when opposed to the communistic abolition of buying and selling, of the bourgeois conditions of production, and the bourgeoisie itself.

You are horrified at our intending to do away with private property. But in your existing society, private property is already done away with for nine tenths of the population; its existence for the few is solely due to its non-existence in the hands of those nine tenths. You reproach us, therefore, with intending to do away with a form of property, the necessary condition for whose existence is the non-existence of any property for the immense majority of society.

In one word, you reproach us with intending to do away with your property. Precisely so; that is just what we intend.

From the moment when labour can no longer be converted into capital, money, or rent, into a social power capable of being monopolized, i.e., from the moment when individual property can no longer be transformed into bourgeois property, into capital, from that moment, you say, individuality vanishes.

You must, therefore, confess that by 'individual' you mean no other person than the bourgeois, than the middle-class owner of property. This person must, indeed, be swept out of the way, and made impossible.

Communism deprives no man of the power to appropriate the products of society; all that it does is to deprive him of the power to subjugate the labour of others by means of such appropriation.

It has been objected that upon the abolition of private property all work will cease, and universal laziness will overtake us.

According to this, bourgeois society ought long ago to have gone to the dogs through sheer idleness; for those of its members who work, acquire nothing, and those who acquire anything, do not work. The whole of this objection is but another expression of the tautology that there can no longer be any wage labour when there is no longer any capital.

All objections urged against the communistic mode of producing and appropriating material products have, in the same way, been urged against the communistic mode of producing and appropriating intellectual products. Just as, to the bourgeois, the disappearance of class property is the disappearance of production itself, so the disappearance of class culture is to him identical with the disappearance of all culture.

That culture, the loss of which he laments, is, for the enormous majority, a mere training to act as a machine.

But don't wrangle with us so long as you apply, to our intended abolition of bourgeois property, the standard of your bourgeois notions of freedom, culture, law, etc. Your very ideas are but the outgrowth of the conditions of your bourgeois production and bourgeois property, just as your jurisprudence is but the will of your class made into a law for all, a will whose essential character and direction are determined by the economical conditions of existence of your class.

The selfish misconception that induces you to transform into eternal laws of nature and of reason the social forms springing from your present mode of production and form of property – historical relations that rise and disappear in the progress of production – this misconception you share with every ruling class that has preceded you. What you see clearly in the case of ancient property, what you admit in the case of feudal property, you are of course forbidden to admit in the case of your own bourgeois form of property.

Abolition of the family! Even the most radical flare up at this infamous proposal of the Communists.

On what foundation is the present family, the bourgeois family, based? On capital, on private gain. In its completely developed form this family exists only among the bourgeoisie. But this state of things finds its complement in the practical absence of the family among the proletarians, and in public prostitution.

The bourgeois family will vanish as a matter of course when its complement vanishes, and both will vanish with the vanishing of capital.

Do you charge us with wanting to stop the exploitation of children by their parents? To this crime we plead guilty.

But, you will say, we destroy the most hallowed of relations, when we replace home education by social.

And your education! Is not that also social, and determined by the social conditions under which you educate, by the intervention direct or indirect, of society, by means of schools, etc.? The Communists have not invented the intervention of society in education; they do but seek to alter the character of that intervention, and to rescue education from the influence of the ruling class.

The bourgeois claptrap about the family and education, about the hallowed co-relation of parent and child, becomes all the more disgusting, the more, by the action of modern industry, all family ties among the proletarians are torn asunder, and their children transformed into simple articles of commerce and instruments of labour.

But you Communists would introduce community of women, screams the whole bourgeoisie in chorus.

The bourgeois sees in his wife a mere instrument of production. He hears that the instruments of production are to be exploited in common, and, naturally, can come to no other conclusion than that the lot of being common to all will likewise fall to the women.

He has not even a suspicion that the real point aimed at is to do away with the status of women as mere instruments of production.

For the rest, nothing is more ridiculous than the virtuous indignation of our bourgeois at the community of women which, they pretend, is to be openly and officially established by the Communists. The Communists have no need to introduce community of women; it has existed almost from time immemorial.

Our bourgeois, not content with having the wives and daughters of their proletarians at their disposal, not to speak of common prostitutes, take the greatest pleasure in seducing each other's wives.

Bourgeois marriage is in reality a system of wives in common, and thus, at the most, what the Communists might possibly be reproached with, is that they desire to introduce, in substitution for a hypocritically concealed, an openly legalized community of women. For the rest, it is self-evident that the abolition of the present system of production must bring with it the abolition of the community of women springing from that system, i.e., of prostitution both public and private.

The Communists are further reproached with desiring to abolish countries and nationality.

The working men have no country. We cannot take from them what they have not got. Since the proletariat must first of all acquire political supremacy, must rise to be the leading class of the nation, must constitute itself as the nation, it is, so far, itself national, though not in the bourgeois sense of the word.

National differences, and antagonisms between peoples, are daily more and more vanishing, owing to the development of the bourgeoisie, to freedom of commerce, to the world market, to uniformity in the mode of production and in the conditions of life corresponding thereto.

The supremacy of the proletariat will cause them to vanish still faster. United action, of the leading civilized countries at least, is one of the first conditions for the emancipation of the proletariat.

In proportion as the exploitation of one individual by another is put an end to, the exploitation of one nation by another will also be put an end to. In proportion as the antagonism between classes within the nation vanishes, the hostility of one nation to another will come to an end.

The charges against communism made from a religious, a philosophical, and, generally, from an ideological standpoint, are not deserving of serious examination.

Does it require deep intuition to comprehend that man's ideas, views and conceptions, in one word, man's consciousness, changes with every change in the conditions of his material existence, in his social relations and in his social life?

What else does the history of ideas prove, than that intellectual production changes its character in proportion as material production is changed? The ruling ideas of each age have ever been the ideas of its ruling class.

When people speak of ideas that revolutionize society, they do but express the fact that within the old society, the elements of a new one have been created, and that the dissolution of the old ideas keeps even pace with the dissolution of the old conditions of existence.

When the ancient world was in its last throes, the ancient religions were overcome by Christianity. When Christian ideas succumbed in the eighteenth century to rationalist ideas, feudal society fought its death battle with the then revolutionary bourgeoisie. The ideas of religious liberty and freedom of conscience merely gave expression to the sway of free competition within the domain of knowledge.

'Undoubtedly,' it will be said, 'religious, moral, philosophical and juridical ideas have been modified in the course of historical development. But religion, morality, philosophy, political science and law constantly survived this change.

'There are, besides, eternal truths, such as freedom, justice, etc., that are common to all states of society. But communism abolishes eternal truths, it abolishes all religion and all morality, instead of constituting them on a new basis; it therefore acts in contradiction to all past historical experience.'

What does this accusation reduce itself to? The history of all past society has consisted in the development of class antagonisms, antagonisms that assumed different forms at different epochs.

But whatever form they may have taken, one fact is common to all past ages, viz., the exploitation of one part of society by the other. No wonder, then, that the social consciousness of past ages, despite all the multiplicity and variety it displays, moves within certain common forms, or general ideas, which cannot completely vanish except with the total disappearance of class antagonisms.

The communist revolution is the most radical rupture with traditional property relations; no wonder that its development involves the most radical rupture with traditional ideas.

But let us have done with the bourgeois objections to communism.

We have seen above, that the first step in the revolution by the working class is to raise the proletariat to the position of ruling class, to win the battle of democracy.

The proletariat will use its political supremacy to wrest, by degrees, all capital from the bourgeoisie, to centralize all instruments of production in the hands of the state, i.e., of the proletariat organized as the ruling class, and to increase the total of productive forces as rapidly as possible.

Of course, in the beginning, this cannot be effected except by means of despotic inroads on the rights of property, and on the conditions of bourgeois production; by means of measures, therefore, which appear economically insufficient and untenable, but which, in the course of the movement, outstrip themselves, necessitate further inroads upon the old social order, and are unavoidable as a means of entirely revolutionizing the mode of production.

These measures will of course be different in different countries.

Nevertheless, in the most advanced countries, the following will be pretty generally applicable:

1.   Abolition of property in land and application of all rents of land to public purposes.
2.   A heavy progressive or graduated income tax.

3. Abolition of all right of inheritance.
4. Confiscation of the property of all emigrants and rebels.
5. Centralization of credit in the hands of the state, by means of a national bank with state capital and an exclusive monopoly.
6. Centralization of the means of communication and transport in the hands of the state.
7. Extension of factories and instruments of production owned by the state; the bringing into cultivation of waste lands, and the improvement of the soil generally in accordance with a common plan.
8. Equal liability of all to labour. Establishment of industrial armies, especially for agriculture.
9. Combination of agriculture with manufacturing industries; gradual abolition of the distinction between town and country, by a more equable distribution of the population over the country.
10. Free education for all children in public schools. Abolition of children's factory labour in its present form. Combination of education with industrial production, etc.

When, in the course of development, class distinctions have disappeared, and all production has been concentrated in the hands of a vast association of the whole nation, the public power will lose its political character. Political power, properly so called, is merely the organized power of one class for oppressing another. If the proletariat during its contest with the bourgeoisie is compelled, by the force of circumstances, to organize itself as a class; if, by means of a revolution, it makes itself the ruling class, and, as such, sweeps away by force the old conditions of production, then it will, along with these conditions, have swept away the conditions for the existence of class antagonisms and of classes generally, and will thereby have abolished its own supremacy as a class.

In place of the old bourgeois society, with its classes and class antagonisms, we shall have an association, in which the free development of each is the condition for the free development of all.

III. Socialist and Communist Literature

1. Reactionary Socialism

a. Feudal Socialism.   Owing to their historical position, it became the vocation of the aristocracies of France and England to write pamphlets against modern bourgeois society. In the French revolution of July 1830, and in the English Reform agitation,[10] these aristocracies again succumbed to the hateful upstart. Thenceforth, a serious political contest was altogether out of question. A literary battle alone remained possible. But even in the domain of literature the old cries of the Restoration period[11] had become impossible.

In order to arouse sympathy, the aristocracy were obliged to lose sight, apparently, of their own interests, and to formulate their indictment against the bourgeoisie in the interest of the exploited working class alone. Thus the aristocracy took their revenge by singing lampoons

---

[10] Of 1830–32.
[11] Not the English Restoration 1660 to 1689, but the French Restoration 1814 to 1830 [Engels].

on their new master, and whispering in his ears sinister prophecies of coming catastrophe.

In this way arose feudal socialism: half lamentation, half lampoon; half echo of the past, half menace of the future; at times, by its bitter, witty and incisive criticism, striking the bourgeoisie to the very heart's core; but always ludicrous in its effect, through total incapacity to comprehend the march of modern history.

The aristocracy, in order to rally the people to them, waved the proletarian alms-bag in front for a banner. But the people, so often as it joined them, saw on their hindquarters the old feudal coats of arms, and deserted with loud and irreverent laughter.

One section of the French Legitimists,[12] and 'Young England',[13] exhibited this spectacle.

In pointing out that their mode of exploitation was different to that of the bourgeoisie, the feudalists forget that they exploited under circumstances and conditions that were quite different, and that are now antiquated. In showing that, under their rule, the modern proletariat never existed, they forget that the modern bourgeoisie is the necessary offspring of their own form of society.

For the rest, so little do they conceal the reactionary character of their criticism that their chief accusation against the bourgeoisie amounts to this, that under the bourgeois regime a class is being developed, which is destined to cut up root and branch the old order of society.

---

[12] The supporters of the restored Bourbon monarchy of 1814–30, representing the landed aristocracy.

[13] A literary circle attached to the Tory party. Benjamin Disraeli's *Sybil: or Two Nations*, and Thomas Carlyle's pamphlets, were among its typical expressions.

What they upbraid the bourgeoisie with is not so much that it creates a proletariat, as that it creates a *revolutionary* proletariat.

In political practice, therefore, they join in all coercive measures against the working class; and in ordinary life, despite their highfalutin phrases, they stoop to pick up the golden apples dropped from the tree of industry, and to barter truth, love, and honour for traffic in wool, beetroot-sugar, and potato spirits.[14]

As the parson has ever gone hand in hand with the landlord, so has clerical socialism with feudal socialism.

Nothing is easier than to give Christian asceticism a socialist tinge. Has not Christianity declaimed against private property, against marriage, against the state? Has it not preached in the place of these, charity and poverty, celibacy and mortification of the flesh, monastic life and Mother Church? Christian socialism is but the holy water with which the priest consecrates the heart-burnings of the aristocrat.

b. Petty-Bourgeois Socialism.   The feudal aristocracy was not the only class that was ruined by the bourgeoisie, not the only class whose conditions of existence pined and perished in the atmosphere of modern bourgeois society. The medieval burgesses and the small peasant proprietors were the precursors of the modern bourgeoisie. In those

---

[14] This applies chiefly to Germany where the landed aristocracy and squirearchy have large portions of their estates cultivated for their own account by stewards, and are, moreover, extensive beetroot-sugar manufacturers and distillers of potato spirits. The wealthier British aristocracy are, as yet, rather above that; but they, too, know how to make up for declining rents by lending their names to floaters of more or less shady joint-stock companies [Engels].

countries which are but little developed, industrially and commercially, these two classes still vegetate side by side with the rising bourgeoisie.

In countries where modern civilization has become fully developed, a new class of petty bourgeois has been formed, fluctuating between proletariat and bourgeoisie and ever renewing itself as a supplementary part of bourgeois society. The individual members of this class, however, are being constantly hurled down into the proletariat by the action of competition, and, as modern industry develops, they even see the moment approaching when they will completely disappear as an independent section of modern society, to be replaced, in manufacture, agriculture and commerce, by overseers, bailiffs, and shop assistants.

In countries like France, where the peasants constitute far more than half of the population, it was natural that writers who sided with the proletariat against the bourgeoisie should use, in their criticism of the bourgeois regime, the standard of the peasant and petty bourgeois, and from the standpoint of these intermediate classes should take up the cudgels for the working class. Thus arose petty-bourgeois socialism. Sismondi[15] was the head of this school, not only in France but also in England.

This school of socialism dissected with great acuteness the contradictions in the conditions of modern production. It laid bare the hypocritical apologies of economists. It proved, incontrovertibly, the disastrous effects of machinery and division of labour; the concentration

---

[15] Sismondi's *Principles of Political Economy* first appeared in 1803.

of capital and land in a few hands; overproduction and crises; it pointed out the inevitable ruin of the petty bourgeois and peasant, the misery of the proletariat, the anarchy in production, the crying inequalities in the distribution of wealth, the industrial war of extermination between nations, the dissolution of old moral bonds, of the old family relations, of the old nationalities.

In its positive aims, however, this form of socialism aspires either to restoring the old means of production and of exchange, and with them the old property relations and the old society, or to cramping the modern means of production and of exchange within the framework of the old property relations that have been, and were bound to be, exploded by those means. In either case, it is both reactionary and utopian.

Its last words are: corporate guilds for manufacture; patriarchal relations in agriculture.

Ultimately, when stubborn historical facts had dispersed all intoxicating effects of self-deception, this form of socialism ended in a miserable fit of the blues.

c. German or 'True' Socialism.   The socialist and communist literature of France, a literature that originated under the pressure of a bourgeoisie in power, and that was the expression of the struggle against this power, was introduced into Germany at a time when the bourgeoisie, in that country, had just begun its contest with feudal absolutism.

German philosophers, would-be philosophers and *beaux esprits* eagerly seized on this literature, only forgetting that when these writings immigrated from France into Germany, French social conditions had not immigrated along with them. In contact with German social conditions, this French literature lost all its immediate practical significance, and assumed a purely literary aspect.[16] Thus, to the German philoso-phers of the eighteenth century, the demands of the first French revolution were nothing more than the demands of 'practical reason' in general, and the utterance of the will of the revolutionary French bour-geoisie signified in their eyes the laws of pure will, of will as it was bound to be, of true human will generally.

The work of the German *literati* consisted solely in bringing the new French ideas into harmony with their ancient philosophical conscience, or rather, in annexing the French ideas without deserting their own philosophic point of view.

This annexation took place in the same way in which a foreign lan-guage is appropriated, namely by translation.

It is well known how the monks wrote silly lives of Catholic saints *over* the manuscripts on which the classical works of ancient heathendom had been written. The German *literati* reversed this process with the profane French literature. They wrote their philosophical nonsense beneath the French original. For instance, beneath the French criticism of the eco-nomic functions of money, they wrote 'alienation of humanity', and beneath the French criticism of the bourgeois state they wrote, 'dethronement of the category of the general', and so forth.

The introduction of these philosophical phrases at the back of the French historical criticisms they dubbed 'philosophy of action', 'true socialism', 'German science of socialism', 'philosophical foundation of socialism', and so on.

[16] In the German editions of the Manifesto there is an additional sentence here which reads (1872): 'It was bound to appear as idle speculation about the real-ization of the essence of man.'

The French socialist and communist literature was thus completely emasculated. And, since it ceased in the hands of the German to express the struggle of one class with the other, he felt conscious of having overcome 'French one-sidedness' and of representing, not true requirements, but the requirements of truth; not the interests of the proletariat, but the interests of human nature, of man in general, who belongs to no class, has no reality, who exists only in the misty realm of philosophical fantasy.

This German socialism, which took its schoolboy task so seriously and solemnly, and extolled its poor stock-in-trade in such mountebank fashion, meanwhile gradually lost its pedantic innocence.

The fight of the German, and especially the Prussian bourgeoisie, against feudal aristocracy and absolute monarchy, in other words, the liberal movement, became more earnest.

By this, the long wished-for opportunity was offered to 'true' socialism of confronting the political movement with the socialist demands, of hurling the traditional anathemas against liberalism, against representative government, against bourgeois competition, bourgeois freedom of the press, bourgeois legislation, bourgeois liberty and equality, and of preaching to the masses that they had nothing to gain, and everything to lose, by this bourgeois movement. German socialism forgot, in the nick of time, that the French criticism, whose silly echo it was, presupposed the existence of modern bourgeois society, with its corresponding economic conditions of existence and the political constitution adapted thereto, the very things whose attainment was the object of the pending struggle in Germany.

To the absolute governments, with their following of parsons, professors, country squires and officials, it served as a welcome scarecrow against the threatening bourgeoisie.

It was a sweet finish after the bitter pills of floggings and bullets with which these same governments, just at that time, dosed the German working-class risings.[17]

While this 'true' socialism thus served the governments as a weapon for fighting the German bourgeoisie, it, at the same time, directly represented a reactionary interest, the interest of the German philistines. In Germany the petty-bourgeois class, a relic of the sixteenth century, and since then constantly cropping up again under various forms, is the real social basis of the existing state of things.

To preserve this class is to preserve the existing state of things in Germany. The industrial and political supremacy of the bourgeoisie threatens it with certain destruction – on the one hand, from the concentration of capital; on the other, from the rise of a revolutionary proletariat. 'True' socialism appeared to kill these two birds with one stone. It spread like an epidemic.

The robe of speculative cobwebs, embroidered with flowers of rhetoric, steeped in the dew of sickly sentiment, this transcendental robe in which the German socialists wrapped their sorry 'eternal truths', all skin and bone, served to wonderfully increase the sale of their goods amongst such a public.

And on its part, German socialism recognized, more and more, its own calling as the bombastic representative of the petty-bourgeois philistine.

It proclaimed the German nation to be the model nation, and the German petty philistine to be the typical man. To every villainous

---

[17] i.e. the Silesian weavers' revolt of 1844.

meanness of this model man it gave a hidden, higher, socialistic interpretation, the exact contrary of its real character. It went to the extreme
length of directly opposing the 'brutally destructive' tendency of communism, and of proclaiming its supreme and impartial contempt of all
class struggles. With very few exceptions, all the so-called socialist and
communist publications that now (1847) circulate in Germany belong to
the domain of this foul and enervating literature.

2. Conservative or Bourgeois Socialism

A part of the bourgeoisie is desirous of redressing social grievances, in
order to secure the continued existence of bourgeois society.

To this section belong economists, philanthropists, humanitarians,
improvers of the condition of the working class, organizers of charity,
members of societies for the prevention of cruelty to animals, tem-
perance fanatics, hole-and-corner reformers of every imaginable kind.
This form of socialism has, moreover, been worked out into complete
systems.

We may cite Proudhon's *Philosophie de la Misère*[18] as an example of this
form.

The socialistic bourgeois want all the advantages of modern social
conditions without the struggles and dangers necessarily resulting
therefrom. They desire the existing state of society minus its revolutionary and disintegrating elements. They wish for a bourgeoisie
without a proletariat. The bourgeoisie naturally conceives the world in

---

[18] It was in reply to Proudhon's *Philosophy of Poverty* (1846) that Marx wrote his
Poverty of Philosophy (1847).

which it is supreme to be the best; and bourgeois socialism develops this comfortable conception into various more or less complete systems. In requiring the proletariat to carry out such a system, and thereby to march straightway into the social New Jerusalem, it but requires in reality that the proletariat should remain within the bounds of existing society, but should cast away all its hateful ideas concerning the bourgeoisie.

A second and more practical, but less systematic, form of this socialism sought to depreciate every revolutionary movement in the eyes of the working class, by showing that no mere political reform, but only a change in the material conditions of existence, in economical relations, could be of any advantage to them. By changes in the material conditions of existence, this form of socialism, however, by no means understands abolition of the bourgeois relations of production, an abolition that can be effected only by a revolution, but administrative reforms, based on the continued existence of these relations; reforms, therefore, that in no respect affect the relations between capital and labour, but, at the best, lessen the cost, and simplify the administrative work, of bourgeois government.

Bourgeois socialism attains adequate expression when, and only when, it becomes a mere figure of speech.

Free trade: for the benefit of the working class. Protective duties: for the benefit of the working class. Prison reform: for the benefit of the working class. This is the last word and the only seriously meant word of bourgeois socialism.

It is summed up in the phrase: the bourgeois is a bourgeois – for the benefit of the working class.

3. Critical-Utopian Socialism and Communism

We do not here refer to that literature which, in every great modern revolution, has always given voice to the demands of the proletariat, such as the writings of Babeuf and others.

The first direct attempts of the proletariat to attain its own ends, made in times of universal excitement, when feudal society was being overthrown, these attempts necessarily failed, owing to the then undeveloped state of the proletariat, as well as to the absence of the economic conditions for its emancipation, conditions that had yet to be produced, and could be produced by the impending bourgeois epoch alone. The revolutionary literature that accompanied these first movements of the proletariat had necessarily a reactionary character. It inculcated universal asceticism and social levelling in its crudest form.

The socialist and communist systems properly so called, those of Saint-Simon, Fourier, Owen and others, spring into existence in the early undeveloped period, described above, of the struggle between proletariat and bourgeoisie (see section I, 'Bourgeoisie and Proletariat').

The founders of these systems see, indeed, the class antagonisms, as well as the action of the decomposing elements in the prevailing form of society. But the proletariat, as yet in its infancy, offers to them the spectacle of a class without any historical initiative or any independent political movement.

Since the development of class antagonism keeps even pace with the development of industry, the economic situation, as they find it, does not as yet offer to them the material conditions for the emancipation of the proletariat. They therefore search after a new social science,[19] after new social laws, that are to create these conditions.

Historical action is to yield to their personal inventive action, historically created conditions of emancipation to fantastic ones, and the gradual, spontaneous class organization of the proletariat to an organization of society specially contrived by these inventors. Future history resolves itself, in their eyes, into the propaganda and the practical carrying out of their social plans.

In the formation of their plans they are conscious of caring chiefly for the interests of the working class, as being the most suffering class. Only from the point of view of being the most suffering class does the proletariat exist for them.

The undeveloped state of the class struggle, as well as their own surroundings, cause socialists of this kind to consider themselves far superior to all class antagonisms. They want to improve the condition of every member of society, even that of the most favoured. Hence, they habitually appeal to society at large, without distinction of class; nay, by preference, to the ruling class. For how can people, when once they understand their system, fail to see in it the best possible plan of the best possible state of society?

Hence, they reject all political, and especially all revolutionary,

---

[19] Here, as in other writings of the 1840s, Marx and Engels still used 'science' in a now archaic sense of the term, roughly equivalent to the modern 'doctrine'. Although the substance of their argument remained the same, the change in usage led them later to refer to their own theory as 'scientific', in contrast to the utopianism of their predecessors. See, for example, Marx's Preface to the first German edition of *Capital*, and Engels's 'Socialism: Utopian and Scientific', both in Marx–Engels, *Selected Works*, Lawrence & Wishart (London 1968).

action; they wish to attain their ends by peaceful means, and endeavour, by small experiments, necessarily doomed to failure, and by the force of example, to pave the way for the new social gospel.

Such fantastic pictures of future society, painted at a time when the proletariat is still in a very undeveloped state and has but a fantastic conception of its own position, correspond with the first instinctive yearnings of that class for a general reconstruction of society.

But these socialist and communist publications contain also a critical element. They attack every principle of existing society. Hence they are full of the most valuable materials for the enlightenment of the working class. The practical measures proposed in them – such as the abolition of the distinction between town and country, of the family, of the carrying on of industries for the account of private individuals, and of the wage system, the proclamation of social harmony, the conversion of the functions of the state into a mere superintendence of production – all these proposals point solely to the disappearance of class antagonisms which were, at the time, only just cropping up, and which, in these publications, are recognized under their earliest, indistinct and undefined forms only. These proposals, therefore, are of a purely utopian character.

The significance of critical-utopian socialism and communism bears an inverse relation to historical development. In proportion as the modern class struggle develops and takes definite shape, this fantastic standing apart from the contest, these fantastic attacks on it, lose all practical value and all theoretical justification. Therefore, although the originators of these systems were, in many respects, revolutionary, their disciples have, in every case, formed mere reactionary sects. They hold fast by the original views of their masters, in opposition to the progressive historical development of the proletariat. They therefore endeavour, and that consistently, to deaden the class struggle and to reconcile the class antagonisms. They still dream of experimental realization of their social utopias, of founding isolated '*phalanstères*', of establishing 'home colonies', of setting up a 'little Icaria'[20] – duodecimo editions of the New Jerusalem – and to realize all these castles in the air, they are compelled to appeal to the feelings and purses of the bourgeois. By degrees they sink into the category of the reactionary conservative socialists depicted above, differing from these only by more systematic pedantry, and by their fanatical and superstitious belief in the miraculous effects of their social science.

They therefore violently oppose all political action on the part of the working class; such action, according to them, can only result from blind unbelief in the new gospel.

The Owenites in England, and the Fourierists in France, respectively oppose the Chartists and the Réformistes.

IV. Position of the Communists in Relation to the Various Existing Opposition Parties

Section II has made clear the relations of the Communists to the existing working-class parties, such as the Chartists in England and the agrarian reformers[21] in America.

---

[20] *Phalanstères* were socialist colonies on the plan of Charles Fourier; Icaria was the name given by Cabet to his utopia and, later on, to his American communist colony [Engels].

[21] This seems to be a reference to the Free Soil movement, which demanded the free distribution of uncultivated land to small farmers.

The Communists fight for the attainment of the immediate aims, for the enforcement of the momentary interests of the working class; but in the movement of the present, they also represent and take care of the future of that movement. In France the Communists ally themselves with the Social-Democrats,[22] against the conservative and radical bourgeoisie, reserving, however, the right to take up a critical position in regard to phrases and illusions traditionally handed down from the great Revolution.

In Switzerland they support the Radicals, without losing sight of the fact that this party consists of antagonistic elements, partly of democratic socialists, in the French sense, partly of radical bourgeois.

In Poland they support the party that insists on an agrarian revolution as the prime condition for national emancipation, that party which fomented the insurrection of Cracow in 1846.

In Germany they fight with the bourgeoisie whenever it acts in a revolutionary way, against the absolute monarchy, the feudal squirearchy, and the petty bourgeoisie.[23]

But they never cease, for a single instant, to instil into the working class the clearest possible recognition of the hostile antagonism between bourgeoisie and proletariat, in order that the German workers may straightway use, as so many weapons against the bourgeoisie, the social and political conditions that the bourgeoisie must necessarily introduce

---

[22] The party then represented in parliament by Ledru-Rollin, in literature by Louis Blanc, in the daily press by *La Réforme*. The name 'Social-Democracy' signified, with these its inventors, a section of the democratic or republican party more or less tinged with socialism [Engels].

[23] *Kleinbürgerei* in the original. 'Petty-bourgeois conditions' would be a more accurate translation.

along with its supremacy, and in order that, after the fall of the reactionary classes in Germany, the fight against the bourgeoisie itself may immediately begin.

The Communists turn their attention chiefly to Germany, because that country is on the eve of a bourgeois revolution that is bound to be carried out under more advanced conditions of European civilization, and with a much more developed proletariat, than that of England was in the seventeenth, and of France in the eighteenth century, and because the bourgeois revolution in Germany will be but the prelude to an immediately following proletarian revolution.

In short, the Communists everywhere support every revolutionary movement against the existing social and political order of things.

In all these movements they bring to the front, as the leading question in each, the property question, no matter what its degree of development at the time.

Finally, they labour everywhere for the union and agreement of the democratic parties of all countries.

The Communists disdain to conceal their views and aims. They openly declare that their ends can be attained only by the forcible overthrow of all existing conditions. Let the ruling classes tremble at a communistic revolution. The proletarians have nothing to lose but their chains. They have a world to win.

WORKING MEN OF ALL COUNTRIES, UNITE!

PREFACE TO THE ENGLISH EDITION OF 1888[1]

Frederick Engels

[1] The preceding translation of the Communist Manifesto was made by Samuel Moore in 1888, and edited by Engels. His notes are identified in this edition by [Engels]. Besides printer's errors, inconsistent and old-fashioned punctuation and orthography, a very few linguistic archaisms have also been amended.

The Manifesto was published as the platform of the Communist League, a working men's association, first exclusively German, later on international, and, under the political conditions of the Continent before 1848, unavoidably a secret society. At a congress of the League, held in London in November 1847, Marx and Engels were commissioned to prepare for publication a complete theoretical and practical party programme. Drawn up in German, in January 1848, the manuscript was sent to the printer in London a few weeks before the French revolution of 24 February. A French translation was brought out in Paris shortly before the insurrection of June 1848. The first English translation, by Miss Helen Macfarlane, appeared in George Julian Harney's *Red Republican*, London, 1850. A Danish and a Polish edition had also been published.

The defeat of the Parisian insurrection of June 1848 – the first great battle between proletariat and bourgeoisie – drove again into the background, for a time, the social and political aspirations of the European working class. Thenceforth, the struggle for supremacy was again, as it had been before the revolution of February, solely between different sections

of the propertied class; the working class was reduced to a fight for political elbow-room, and to the position of extreme wing of the middle-class
radicals. Wherever independent proletarian movements continued to
show signs of life, they were ruthlessly hunted down. Thus the Prussian
police hunted out the Central Board[2] of the Communist League, then
located in Cologne. The members were arrested, and, after eighteen
months' imprisonment, they were tried in October 1852. This celebrated
'Cologne Communist Trial' lasted from 4 October till 12 November;
seven of the prisoners were sentenced to terms of imprisonment in a
fortress, varying from three to six years. Immediately after the sentence,
the League was formally dissolved by the remaining members. As to the
Manifesto, it seemed thenceforth to be doomed to oblivion.

When the European working class had recovered sufficient strength for
another attack on the ruling classes, the International Working Men's
Association sprang up. But this association, formed with the express aim of
welding into one body the whole militant proletariat of Europe and
America, could not at once proclaim the principles laid down in the
Manifesto. The International was bound to have a programme broad
enough to be acceptable to the English trade unions, to the followers of
Proudhon in France, Belgium, Italy and Spain, and to the Lassalleans[3] in
Germany. Marx, who drew up this programme to the satisfaction of all
parties, entirely trusted to the intellectual development of the working

---

[2] i.e. the Central Committee, as it is referred to elsewhere.
[3] Lassalle personally, to us, always acknowledged himself to be a disciple of Marx,
and, as such, stood on the ground of the Manifesto. But in his public agitation,
1862–64, he did not go beyond demanding cooperative workshops supported by
state credit [Engels].

class, which was sure to result from combined action and mutual discussion. The very events and vicissitudes of the struggle against capital, the defeats even more than the victories, could not help bringing home to men's minds the insufficiency of their various favourite nostrums, and preparing the way for a more complete insight into the true conditions of working-class emancipation. And Marx was right. The International, on its breaking up in 1874,[4] left the workers quite different men from what it had found them in 1864. Proudhonism in France, Lassalleanism in Germany were dying out, and even the conservative English trade unions, though most of them had long since severed their connection with the International, were gradually advancing towards that point at which, last year at Swansea, their President could say in their name, 'Continental socialism has lost its terrors for us.'[5] In fact: the principles of the Manifesto had made considerable headway among the working men of all countries.

The Manifesto itself thus came to the front again. The German text had been, since 1850, reprinted several times in Switzerland, England and America. In 1872, it was translated into English in New York, where the translation was published in *Woodhull and Claflin's Weekly*.[6] From this

[4]   In fact the International was not officially wound up until 1876, although it effectively ceased to function when the General Council was transferred to New York in 1972.

[5]   W. Bevan, in his address to the TUC Congress, reported in the *Commonweal*, 17 September 1887.

[6]   This paper was published by two American feminists, Victoria Woodhull and her sister Tennessee Claflin, whose campaign Marx considered 'middle-class humbug' and who were eventually expelled from the International. See International Working Men's Association, *Documents of the First International*, Lawrence & Wishart (London 1964–66), pp. 323–32. It carried an abridged translation of the Manifesto on 30 December 1871.

English version, a French one was made in *Le Socialiste* of New York. Since then at least two more English translations, more or less mutilated, have been brought out in America, and one of them has been reprinted in England. The first Russian translation, made by Bakunin, was published at Herzen's *Kolokol*[7] office in Geneva, about 1863; a second one, by the heroic Vera Zasulich,[8] also in Geneva, 1882. A new Danish edition is to be found in *Socialdemokratisk Bibliothek*, Copenhagen, 1885; a fresh French translation in *Le Socialiste*, Paris, 1885. From this latter a Spanish version was prepared and published in Madrid, 1886. The German reprints are not to be counted, there have been twelve altogether at the least. An Armenian translation, which was to be published in Constantinople some months ago, did not see the light, I am told, because the publisher was afraid of bringing out a book with the name of Marx on it, while the translator declined to call it his own production. Of further translations into other languages I have heard, but have not seen them. Thus the history of the Manifesto reflects, to a great extent, the history of the modern working-class movement; at present it is undoubtedly the most widespread, the most international production of all socialist literature, the common platform acknowledged by millions of working men from Siberia to California.

Yet, when it was written, we could not have called it a 'Socialist' manifesto. By 'socialists', in 1847, were understood, on the one hand, the

---

[7]   Alexander Herzen was a Russian philosopher and revolutionary democrat. His paper *Kolokol* (The Bell) was the leading organ of the Russian emigration in the 1860s. Bakunin's translation of the Manifesto was in fact published in 1869.

[8]   Engels celebrates Vera Zasulich for her attempted assassination of the governor of St Petersburg, General Trepov, in 1878. The translation was in fact by George Plekhanov, the founder of Russian Marxism.

adherents of the various utopian systems: Owenites in England, Fourierists in France, both of them already reduced to the position of mere sects, and gradually dying out; on the other hand, the most multifarious social quacks, who, by all manners of tinkering, professed to redress, without any danger to capital and profit, all sorts of social grievances; in both cases men outside the working-class movement, and looking rather to the 'educated' classes for support. Whatever portion of the working class had become convinced of the insufficiency of mere political revolutions, and had proclaimed the necessity of a total social change, that portion then called itself communist. It was a crude, rough-hewn, purely instinctive sort of communism; still, it touched the cardinal point and was powerful enough amongst the working class to produce the utopian communism, in France, of Cabet, and in Germany, of Weitling. Thus, socialism was, in 1847, a middle-class movement, communism a working-class movement. Socialism was, on the Continent at least, 'respectable'; communism was the very opposite. And as our notion, from the very beginning, was that 'the emancipation of the working class must be the act of the working class itself', there could be no doubt as to which of the two names we must take. Moreover, we have, ever since, been far from repudiating it.

The Manifesto being our joint production, I consider myself bound to state that the fundamental proposition, which forms its nucleus, belongs to Marx. That proposition is: that in every historical epoch, the prevailing mode of economic production and exchange, and the social organization necessarily following from it, form the basis upon which is built up, and from which alone can be explained, the political and intellectual history of that epoch; that consequently the whole history of mankind (since the dissolution of primitive tribal society, holding land in common ownership) has been a history of class struggles, contests between exploiting and exploited, ruling and oppressed classes; that the history of these class struggles forms a series of evolutions in which, nowadays, a stage has been reached where the exploited and oppressed class – the proletariat – cannot attain its emancipation from the sway of the exploiting and ruling class – the bourgeoisie – without, at the same time, and once and for all, emancipating society at large from all exploitation, oppression, class distinctions and class struggles.

This proposition which, in my opinion, is destined to do for history what Darwin's theory has done for biology, we, both of us, had been gradually approaching for some years before 1845. How far I had independently progressed towards it is best shown by my *Condition of the Working Class in England*. But when I again met Marx at Brussels, in spring 1845, he had it ready worked out, and put it before me, in terms almost as clear as those in which I have stated it here.

From our joint preface to the German edition of 1872, I quote the following:

However much the state of things may have altered during the last twenty-five years, the general principles laid down in this Manifesto are, on the whole, as correct today as ever. Here and there some detail might be improved. The practical application of the principles will depend, as the Manifesto itself states, everywhere and at all times, on the historical conditions for the time being existing, and, for that reason, no special stress is laid on the revolutionary measures proposed at the end of section II. That passage would, in many respects, be very differently worded today. In view of the gigantic strides of modern industry since 1848, and of the accompanying improved and extended organization of the working class; in view of the practical experience gained, first in the February revolution, and then, still more, in the Paris Commune, where the proletariat for the first time held political power for two whole months, this programme has in some details become antiquated. One thing especially was proved by the Commune, viz., that 'the working class cannot simply lay hold of the ready-made state machinery, and wield it for its own purposes'. (See 'The Civil War in France', section III, where this point is further developed.) Further, it is self-evident that the criticism of socialist literature is deficient in relation to the present time, because it comes down only to 1847; also, that the remarks on the relation of the Communists to the various opposition parties (section IV), although in principle still correct, yet in practice are antiquated, because the political situation has been entirely changed, and the progress of history has swept from off the earth the greater portion of the political parties there enumerated.

But then, the Manifesto has become a historical document which we have no longer any right to alter.

The present translation is by Mr Samuel Moore, the translator of the greater portion of Marx's *Capital*. We have revised it in common, and I have added a few notes explanatory of historical allusions.

London, 30 January 1888